NAILED IT!
10 Keys to Crushing the Interview

Powerful & Practical!

*Advanced Strategies and Techniques to nail your next interview
and get the job or promotion you desire most*

MATTHEW G. MARVIN
(Owner/President/Speaker/Consultant/
Executive Coach at MGM Consulting)

Foreword by Keith Lawrence
(Former P&G HR Executive, Peak Performance Consultant
and Co-Author of the Amazon Top 1% Best Selling Book
Your Retirement Quest)

DEDICATION

First and foremost, I want to thank God, who makes all things possible. It was His inspiration that made the pages of this book a reality.

To my wife, Tammy, who was so patient with me as I worked many nights and weekends to complete this project. I love you and I am forever grateful for you. To my daughter, Caila, and my son, Cole, who are constant sources of inspiration. I am so blessed to be your dad. To my mom, who taught me the power of faith and persistence. Mom, I am so grateful to be your son. And to all my family and friends who have always been there for me with constant and never wavering support. You mean the world to me and I thank God every day for each and every one of you. I am blessed to have you all in my life.

CONTENTS

TESTIMONIALS

"I have experienced the impact of *"Nailed it"* from both the interviewer and the interviewee side and have witnessed the impact of the strategy Matthew teaches as well as seen the confidence of those that have participated in his workshops. It has had an amazing impact, both for me personally and for those associates that have taken the opportunity to attend Matt's workshops. I would highly recommend the *Nailed It* concepts to anyone who will face an interview in the future."

Jeff Abate
Vice President of Retail Operations
The Kroger Company
Cincinnati, OH

"MGM Consulting (Matthew Marvin) has been instrumental in preparing our NFL draft prospects for the biggest job interview of their life at the NFL Combine in Indianapolis. His expertise in interviewing skills training is both outstanding and professional. We are blessed to have him as part of our program here at Ignition APG."

Clif Marshall
Performance Director
Ignition Athletic Performance Group
Cincinnati, Ohio

"Let's face it – interviewing for a job intimidates most of us. 'Nailed It' by Matthew will get you past your fears, completely prepare you for interviews, and set you up for success. All you will need to do is execute on his advice. Matthew's vast experience in the field of recruitment for top organizations will give you insights and best practices to equip you to make the best possible impression with decision makers. If you want to get it right, 'Nailed It' will put you on the right path to powerful interviewing."

Steve Biondo
SVP Human Resources and Organizational Development
Family Christian Stores
Grand Rapids, Michigan

"I had the pleasure of working with Matt in our graduate program in human resource development at Xavier University. His creativity, intelligence and caring nature helped his fellow classmates and professors learn greatly from his experience. He has been a regular guest lecturer in the program as an alumnus, and the students always appreciate his energy, ideas and enthusiasm. This book serves as a wonderful blueprint for our students investigating new jobs or new careers."

Dr. Brenda S. Levya-Gardner
Associate Professor & Director
Xavier University
Human Resource Development Graduate Program
Cincinnati, Ohio

"Using the interviewing skills articulated in Nailed It will definitely help you land that next great job! It helps you prepare, deliver and answer all those tough interviewing questions. Nailed It will provide you with the confidence and techniques you need to 'nail' the job you deserve!"

Cathy Gellenbeck
Former Associate Director
University of Cincinnati - Center for Corporate Learning
Cincinnati, Ohio

"Matt brings positive energy and a passion for helping others to all of his interactions and he has presented as a guest speaker numerous times as an alumus. Matt's creativity and wealth of experience in human resources is exemplified in this practical book that will be a valuable resource for all job seekers!"

Dr. Sharon Korth
Associate Professor
Xavier University
Human Resource Development Graduate Program
Cincinnati, Ohio

"Matthew Marvin outlines a clear and accessible road map for anyone who wants to not only improve but excel in their interviewing skills. I would recommend this book to candidates preparing for an interview in any field."

Heather Maloney
Library Director & Associate Senior Librarian
University of Cincinnati
Blue Ash, Ohio

"This book has done more to properly prepare candidates for those crucial interviews than anything else I've experienced in my career. It provides simple, but incredibly effective tips that allow the candidate to shine and present their best possible case to the interviewer."

Ed Taylor
Director, Retail Ops – Shrink Management
The Kroger Company
Cincinnati, OH

"I learned so much from these interviewing strategies and I feel like it is the reason why I have achieved success in obtaining my position to this day. These tips will help me for the rest of my life."

John Hughes
Defensive Lineman
Cleveland Browns

"I have been in Retail Management for over 30 years and thought that I had seen good books, classes and seminars on interviewing. None have been as insightful, purposeful and actionable as *Nailed it*. The *Nailed it* concepts taught by Matthew Marvin have been a game changer for me and my career.

Framing, Passion, the Stacking Effect – each of these aspects provide new-found tools and confidence for the interviewing process."

John Minea
Area Manager
The Kroger Company
Cincinnati, Ohio

"After 28 years with P&G, I decided to retire early. With the confidence that comes form leaving at a high point in my career, I was shaken when after several interviews I found myself finishing 2nd or 3rd among other interviewing candidates. I decided to have an interviewing expert like Matthew teach me real winning strategies. His help was just what I needed when I needed it. After learning and implementing the concepts outlined in this book, I landed the role of Director with one of the largest IT Consulting Firms in the world! I would recommend this book to all my professional friends and colleagues."

Patrick Nelson
Former Director of Global Business Services at P&G
Now Practice Director, Manufacturing Operations
Tara Consultancy Services
Cincinnati, OH

"Taking your interviews to the next level ... this book provides an approach to improve your outline, preparation, and delivery. It will also prepare you to answer the tough questions, which most interviewees struggle to answer, with confidence. Application of the concepts will leave you and your interviewer saying ... "Nailed It!"

James Giebler
Retail Operations Manager
The Kroger Company
Cincinnati, Ohio

"At the end of the day in an interview, you have to be yourself. But the things that Matthew Marvin teaches you about interviewing with the *Nailed It* concepts help you to show the best parts of who you are. The skills I developed from his interviewing prep really helped me to be prepared for the tough questions that NFL GMs, Owners, Coordinators and Coaches ask. I loved the feeling of being confident in how I was going to answer questions because I had practiced them already."

Jackson Jeffcoat
Linebacker
Washington Redskins

"Outstanding, practical instruction–a great value & worth the read. Truly able to take interviewing skills to the next level. Anyone following this advice will most certainly be amazed at their improvement "

Lynne Rudd
Human Resources Manager
The Kroger Company
Cincinnati, Ohio

"Working with Matthew and the concepts in this book helped me to be completely prepared for (and confident with) my interviews heading into the NFL Combine. Matthew's coaching and the interviewing strategies outlined in this book helped me to know everything I can expect in the interview process and prepared to handle anything that gets thrown at me."

Kyle Christy
Punter (NFL Free Agent)
Florida Gators
Gainesville, Florida

"As a young professional in the workplace, professional growth and development is extremely important. With Matt's *10 Keys to Crushing the Interview*, I've been given the tools necessary to get to the next level in my career. Matt, who is a trusted and well-respected consultant at many Fortune 500 companies (including mine) was able to help me identify the behaviors that may have held me back from previous opportunities. But not only that, the *10 Keys to Crushing the Interview* has allowed me to master my delivery to common (and uncommon) interview questions — I am more confident, self-aware and most importantly, extremely **prepared**. *Nailed It* provides the proper coaching techniques and fundamentals everyone needs to land their dream job and I will *never* interview without these strategies again."

Brittney French
Training & Development Manager
The Kroger Company
Cincinnati, OH

"As a junior in college, I had an interview with ZS Associates ranked as the 5th hardest job interview by *Business Insider*. Thanks to the coaching I received from Matthew Marvin, I was able to nail the interview, secure an internship, and land an eventual full time consulting position before my Senior year of college began! His coaching helped me to feel confident and prepared for every question or situation I would face. His knowledge and constant encouragement gave me the feeling I would land the position before the interview even took place."

Blake Avery
Graduate of Washington University
Consultant
ZS Associates
Chicago, Illinois

"I never thought interviewing could actually be fun! These are skills I will take with me the rest of my career–Thank You!"

Sarah Balemian
Corporate Labor Manager
The Kroger Company
Cincinnati, Ohio

"I was selected for an interview with Gatton Academy at Western Kentucky University, which is considered by most experts to be the number one high school in America. I had wanted this for years but was dreading interview day. The concepts and strategies in this book made interview day actually enjoyable! I went in with confidence and 'nailed it!'"

Ethan Abate
Junior in High School & Member of Mensa
Gatton Academy of Mathematics & Science
Bowling Green, Kentucky

"Three people from my team have used these interviewing strategies and have been promoted within our company over the course of the last few months ... and I am one them. I interviewed for a position in Portland that is a couple levels above my current pay grade and I *nailed it!* Thanks for the positive difference that these strategies make!"

Reba Phillips
KCAC Manager
The Kroger Company
Portland, Oregon

"During my second year of grad school at Xavier University, I had the opportunity to attend one of Matthew's seminars on advanced interviewing techniques and my eyes were opened. It was at the seminar where I learned how to compete for those high paying jobs and I knew that my future would be different from then on. Using the *Nailed It* concepts, I was able to get the first job I interviewed for out of grad school and negotiate a 25% increase in salary for that job. I would highly recommend *Nailed It* for anyone as it would change their career trajectory for the better."

Brandon Elmer
Project Manager
Val Verde Regional Medical Center
Del Rio, Texas

"I recommend these techniques for anyone going into a high level interview because it will help you gain the skills and confidence to stand out amongst your peers."

Nicholas Lander
Physician Practice Executive
Seton Healthcare Family
Austin, Texas

FOREWORD

⟢

T he well-known author Jim Collins captured in his best selling book _Good to Great_ that the world's best companies focus first on getting the right people on the bus in the right seats. This sounds simple doesn't it? But any leader who has tried to do this knows this is a very challenging and never-ending task. How do you screen from the thousands of applicants and identify those who should join your team? This decision you make could very well determine if your business has a phenomenal year (or struggles to meet it's goals).

The "Thomas Edison" of our times (Steve Jobs) talked about how "interviewing is a collaborative process". Based on my experience in recruiting hundreds of people, I couldn't agree more. Both stakeholders in this process play a critical role–the candidate and the interviewer. During my thirty-two years at Procter & Gamble, we recognized this–with extensive training for those who would hit the college campuses seeking great talent. We sharpened and honed their interviewing skills to a science.

What about the candidate? What do they do to prepare themselves to best present what they have to offer? In most cases, it is the "trial by error" approach. Take enough swings at the bat and sooner or later you'll become better, right?. Unfortunately, in the meantime, you waste a lot of time and potentially miss that perfect opportunity as you bomb one of your early interviews.

Matthew Marvin has gleaned from his decades of experience in business the ten secrets to nailing the interview. No more "hit or miss". This is a proven approach of strategies and techniques that help candidates present "their very best self". His insights are practical, powerful, and help individuals separate themselves from the rest of the pack. Matthew has proven that his approach works–with college graduates, athletes interviewing for professional opportunities, and experienced executive leaders who are seeking new assignments.

I know, first hand, how well Matthew's unique interviewing methodology works. This summer, he coached one of our daughters who was seeking a new job opportunity in his techniques. In every situation where she landed an interview, she was offered a position with the firm. While I would like to believe it was because of Jennifer's credentials, there is no doubt (in her mind and mine) that she couldn't have achieved this level of success in the interviewing process without using Matthew's interviewing strategies and what he calls the "Stacking Effect". His deep caring and passion for helping others "be their very best" has enabled him to develop a system that will allow you to do the same.

Today's business environment is hyper competitive. Great talent is in short supply. Companies cannot afford to waste time in deciding whom best to join their team. In addition, individuals seeking the next great adventure in their life need to "Nail" every interviewing opportunity they receive. It is your turn to win the interviewing game. This is a book whose time has truly come.

Keith Lawrence
Former P&G HR Executive
Peak Performance Consultant and Co-Author of the Amazon Top 1%
Best Selling Book *Your Retirement Quest*

INTRODUCTION

Regardless of where you are in the interview process (whether you have been in business for twenty years or you are getting ready to interview for your first job right out of college), the *advanced* interviewing techniques and strategies in this book will have a profound positive impact on your results. The solutions in this book are proven strategies that have helped individuals that range from senior business executives, professional athletes, college graduates, organizational managers, and entry level professionals. Whether you are preparing for a promotional opportunity, seeking an athletic career with a professional team, interested in obtaining a new job with a different company, or just starting your career search straight out of college, this book is for you. Each solution is a proven strategy for *nailing* some of the most common (and most challenging) interview questions. We will take the most commonly asked questions in the interview process today and share the best way to frame up your answer to ensure you are able to effectively reply with power and poise. The Bottom Line ... It is time for you to <u>Nail</u> your next interview and acquire the job or promotion you most desire. This book is designed to help you do just that.

Many people head into the interview process believing they have done everything they can to ensure they will perform well in the interview.

They research the hiring company on the Internet, carefully read the job description, and review the requirements for the role. From the information they gather, they then prepare some intelligent questions to ask the interviewer. Candidates often share with me that they also understand the importance of dressing professionally, giving a good firm handshake, and looking the interviewer in the eye. All of these things I just mentioned are important and we certainly encourage interviewers to do them all. However, the problem with these interviewing tips is the fact that this is what *EVERYONE* does! While important, these steps do not separate a candidate from the pack of other viable candidates.

At MGM Consulting, we consider these, and the majority of other tips that can often be found on the Internet, to be "basic" interviewing techniques. While we will address some of these briefly in this book, we have devoted the majority of this content to <u>advanced</u> interviewing strategies that will absolutely cause you to stand out from the crowd. We want to help you *nail* the interview process and be considered the best candidate for the position that you seek. Candidates who use the techniques outlined in this book not only distinguish themselves as master-interviewers, but also often find that they are often offered the job even amidst candidates who may be more experienced and perhaps more applicable for the role.

**Wherever you are in your career, one thing is for certain;
You must be armed with the best skills available to ensure you
<u>Nail</u> the interview and get the job you desire most.**

Have you ever interviewed with an organization, really connected with the interviewer and felt you did well, only to never hear from the organization again? People tell us of similar experiences all the time. They attend interviewing skills workshops at their schools, universities, or organizations and look up a few things on the Internet. However, for some reason, no matter how hard they prepare for the interview, they are not selected as the top candidate for the position. Some professionals share their experiences of having done well interviewing earlier in their career and successfully acquired the position they were interviewing for, but now realize that as they advance to higher levels within the organization, the same interviewing skills that helped them to successfully win the interview in the past may no longer help them in the interview process for higher-level professional and executive roles today.

There are also many people in the aging workforce today that are having the experience of being downsized or "rightsized" from organizations and these job seekers now find themselves having to compete with younger, more technically-savvy candidates and are in need of every edge they can get in the interview process. There are also professionals who have worked as individual contributors in their current or previous roles who now need to ensure they are well prepared for the promotional interviewing questions they will be asked to determine if they are properly suited to move to the next level and lead others. Recent college graduates, after working hard to complete their education and after paying upwards of a hundred thousand dollars to acquire their degree, are finding that in order to acquire their desired job, they may be competing with other more educated and experienced professionals. They quickly realize their desperate need for advanced interviewing strategies to compete effectively in the job market.

This book is designed to provide you with strategies for answering some of the most commonly asked questions in the interview that often make or break a candidate's opportunity for acquiring the position. These are not basic interviewing suggestions. Rather, this book is packed with advanced strategies and time-tested interviewing solutions that will help you to nail your very next interview. Do not leave your future to chance. Take charge of the interviewing opportunities in your life and obtain the position you most desire.

Here's to Your Success!

"The Stacking Effect"

—◦◦◦—

Many people read an interviewing skills book for one of two primary reasons. It is usually either out of inspiration ... or desperation. Some have experienced the great feelings associated with doing pretty well in an interview (we are inspired to learn additional insights that can take our interviewing skills to an even greater level). Some, conversely, have also experienced the pit in the stomach after walking out of an interview knowing that we "botched" it completely (out of desperation, we never want to experience that feeling again). I have great news! The wisdom you will learn from this book is the answer to both of these scenarios. My company has researched the field of interviewing and discovered a formula for success in the interview process that is effective for every field in which we consult (from executive level professionals to college graduates, from candidates applying for a role in a new organization to company associates applying for an internal promotion, and from professional athletes interviewing for the opportunity of a lifetime to teachers who are looking for a new school district). These interviewing strategies flat out work in all fields and help candidates to *Nail* their interviews and get the job they deserve.

I have a lot of passion for helping people to learn and apply these advanced interviewing strategies. I have witnessed the impact of putting

23

these practical techniques for winning the interview to work. Countless individuals who performed poorly in the interview process in the past and had fallen into the trap of believing they were destined for less than they desired have now broken through barriers and achieved great success. Let me be clear on one thing;

You should absolutely nail every interview for which you have effectively prepared!

I absolutely believe that if you have worked hard, gained experience, and have received the knowledge and skills to do the job for which you are applying, you should absolutely nail every interview you participate in and receive an offer for the role. I often have professionals approach me to enquire about advanced interviewing skills. In the course of our conversation, I will ask about their last interviewing experience. They start with the statement, "well, it went....o.k." They then go on to generally explain that they felt they were prepared for the interview and that they felt a good connection with the interviewer. However, time and time again, when they finally get to the point that they did not get the job, they frequently say the words, "maybe it just was not meant to be." For me, hearing this statement is like hearing fingernails on a chalkboard. Let me explain why.

First, there is a psychological component to this statement. In effect, it is a way for this person to release themselves from any responsibility for a failed interview. If they can convince themselves that "maybe it just was not meant to be," then they do not have to feel that they personally did anything wrong. "I was prepared....but it just was not meant to be," they tell themselves. The most dangerous effect of this statement is that it often prevents the candidate from ever taking steps to more effectively preparing for future interviews.

If a candidate convinces themselves that "it just was not meant to be," what will they change about their approach to the interview? The answer: absolutely nothing! Why should they? After all, "it just was not meant to be" and if that is the case, what could they have done to change *fate*? Because this candidate provides themselves with the psychological relief from any responsibility for not getting the job, they will not change their general approach to interviewing. The reason this troubles me is that this same person will suddenly discover it "was not meant to be" for their next several consecutive interviews and will find themselves quickly embracing the belief that perhaps they were "destined" to have an unfulfilling, lower paying career than they truly deserve or desire (and that is a tragedy).

Secondly, I have worked with countless professionals who have worked very hard since their youth to ensure they are ready for the career they are most excited to obtain. The amount of time, energy, and money that is spent in schooling, college, post-graduate and doctoral programs is staggering. According to the National Center for Education Statistics and their published "2013 Digest of Education Statistics," the average cost of a four-year degree (tuition, fees, room & board) is over $23,872 per year. That's an education cost of over $95,000 dollars if they are fortunate enough to complete their coursework within four years (many college students take five years or more to obtain an undergraduate degree). Many people have accumulated over 12–16 years of schooling and tens of thousands of dollars in college loans. Did you know that the average time it takes to pay off a student loan is 22 years? Twenty Two!

The most shocking part of all of this, though, is that our personal research revealed the following.

The average length of time candidates spend preparing for an interview that will potentially impact the trajectory of their entire career ... is thirty minutes!

My personal research supports that over 70% of this thirty minute prep time is actually spent on researching factoids about the company, reviewing their resume, and simply thinking about how they might answer some of the questions that might arise. As a result, my reply to those who tell me, "Maybe it just was not meant to be" is:

"Let me get this straight. You have spent over sixteen years in elementary, high school, and college; you have tens of thousands of dollars in student loans that will take you more than two decades to pay back; and you have spent a whopping 30 minutes preparing for the interview of your life in hopes to obtain the job that will determine your future career ... and when you discovered that you did not get the job, you dare to state, 'Maybe it just was not meant to be.' Are you kidding me?!"

So, let me just come right out and say it.

You have worked way too long and way too hard NOT to get the job that you most desire. Period!

Would you like to know, then, what is "meant to be?" I'll tell you what is "meant to be." What is "meant to be" is that after twelve to sixteen plus years spent on your education and tens of thousands of dollars in educational costs and loans, you should be able to walk into any interview and absolutely nail it! After all the work that you have done to prepare for your career, what is "meant to be" is for you to nail every single interview and the biggest challenge you should be facing is how to select from all the job offers that you have received. THAT is what is "meant to be." And I have good news. You can do just that!

I have developed a formula for interviewing that helps candidates perform with far greater success rates. Candidates who use these techniques stand "head & shoulders" above their competitors. It is a formula that is practical and powerful and will help candidates obtain positions that they may have been unable to secure in the past. How? It is through a process I call "The Stacking Effect." And the best news of all is this:

The interviewing techniques in this book can easily be learned and incorporated into your next interview.

Through "The Stacking Effect," you will achieve real results fast and gain a very positive reaction from your interviewers. I have developed a way for you to win the interview game. After countless interviews with candidates that range from entry-level professionals to senior executives, I have unlocked the power of utilizing each of the techniques referenced in this book throughout the interview process to create an experience for the interviewer that we call "The Stacking Effect." Here is how it works. When a candidate does or says something effectively in an interview, it is as if a "plus sign" is added next to their name on the interviewer's mental candidate chart. Throughout the interview process, interviewers score each candidate by making mental "plusses" and "minuses" and essentially adding up the two columns to see which candidate "wins." While this process is not often completed consciously by the interviewer but subconsciously through their mental evaluations of each candidate, "The Stacking Effect" is already in motion. Rest assured, these mental "plusses" and "minuses" most definitely add up!

Candidates who leverage the techniques outlined in this book will have a clear advantage over other candidates when interviewing for the same position. As their "plusses" stack up, it becomes quite obvious that this candidate is not only ideal for the role, but that the interviewer would miss out on a golden opportunity to employ an amazing candidate if they do not hire them. It is at this point that "The Stacking Effect" is in full force and the candidate quickly gains the favor of the interviewing panel. "The Stacking Effect" is powerful for any given candidate. It becomes even more evident when the interviewing panel members are interviewing candidates back-to-back. Like the balances of a scale, the "plusses" for the candidate who leverages the interviewing tips in this book become even more evident compared to candidates who use basic interviewing skills to simply survive the interviewing process. By leveraging "The Stacking Effect," candidates often find that the "plusses" they receive through the interview process often "tip" the scale in their favor.

The "Stacking Effect" has five levels. These levels stack upward like the layers of a pyramid (see graphic).

The "Stacking Effect"

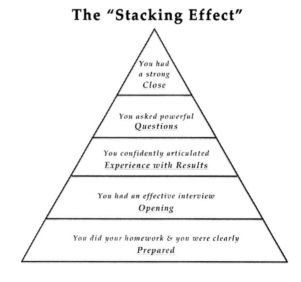

LAYER 1: Preparation

Preparation is the foundation of "The Stacking Effect," upon which all other layers rest. In this book, we provide you with a comprehensive, proactive approach to effectively preparing for the interview.

LAYER 2: Effectively Opening the Interview

There is a question that is asked in almost every interview that trips up candidates without them even knowing it! We have an entire chapter devoted to appropriately and effectively opening the interview in such a way that it provides a lasting, positive impression with the interviewer. This technique helps to launch the interview in a favorable direction for the candidate.

LAYER 3: Confidently Articulating Your Experience With Results

The third layer is where the "body" of the interview takes place. We will teach you how to best share your experiences throughout the interview to pique the interest of the interviewers and leave them wanting to hear more about you, your skills & your experiences.

LAYER 4: Asking Powerful Questions

Most people make the terrible mistake of asking intelligent questions at the end of the interview. Yes, I said "mistake" and it should be with a capital "M." We will share with you why simply asking "intelligent questions" is a mistake and how you can really separate yourself from other highly qualified candidates by asking the *right* questions. The question asking technique that we share with you will clearly separate you from the crowd and leave you standing out as the absolute best candidate for the position!

LAYER 5: A Strong Close

Candidates will often run the interviewing race well only to trip at the finish line! We have talked with employers and candidates alike that have experienced interviews during which candidates have been "winning" the entire interview only to poorly close the interview and fail to get the job. Do not trip ten feet in front of the finish line! There are certain words and phrases that should NEVER be uttered in the closing moments of an interview. We will teach you those phrases so you never trip over them again. We will also teach you a powerful and practical technique for closing the interview. This technique is so powerful that interviewers will see you as their strongest candidate, brag about you and all your greatest qualities, and remember you long after the interview is over.

These five layers of the pyramid culminate to create "The Stacking Effect," which is a powerful way to absolutely nail the job interview and obtain the career of your dreams. While it is important to understand each layer of the pyramid, it is also critical that you understand the challenges being faced by your future employers and know how to think like the interviewer.

BEHAVIORAL-BASED INTERVIEWING

John felt he was well prepared for anything the interviewers might throw at him. He stayed up for hours the night before doing a Google search on the organization and writing down all the specific details that would make him appear bright, professional, and prepared. He thoroughly reviewed the responsibilities of the job to ensure he knew what was required for the position. He contemplated some intelligent questions he could ask and wrote them down to show he had done his homework and was well prepared. He made extra copies of his resume, which were printed on expensive parchment paper, and purchased a leather portfolio containing a forty-dollar pen and a clean white paper pad for taking notes. His five hundred dollar suit was pressed, his tie had a perfect dimple, and his shoes were freshly polished. The night before the interview, John even had his best friend ask him a few questions that he might be asked in the interview so he could practice his answers. When John entered the conference room for his initial interview the next morning, he felt strong and confident.

As the interviewers entered the room, John stood up and gave each one a firm handshake. He smiled and said, "Thanks for the opportunity to interview for this position." Everyone was smiling and they enjoyed some idle "chit-chat" at the start of the interview. John noticed this informal dialogue continued for nearly ten minutes as they all seemed to be having fun, laughing and enjoying their time together. He felt connected and well liked and was sure he had already won them over. They continued to ask him general high-level questions like, "How are you doing?"; "Great weather we are having, isn't it?"; and "Tell me about yourself?" With every answer, they smiled, nodded, and wrote many notes on the documents in front of them. John was convinced that everything was going very well (certainly they would not be so positive if they did not like his answers).

John connected so well with them that there was never a need to open his leather binder, reference his resume, or take any notes. Half way through the interview, he felt that now opening his binder would make him appear unprepared. John wanted to keep the good vibe flowing and stay focused by speaking "off-the-cuff." He was a little surprised when they asked several questions about his experience. "Tell me about a time when you did similar work to this in the past," one interviewer asked him. "In the past, how have you handled employees who became disgruntled?," another enquired. His resume clearly reflected the fact that while he had gained good experience with his previous employers, he did not have much experience in this particular line of work. Undeterred, John confidently shared what he *would* do in the new role and how he *would* handle those situations if they ever came up in the future. Again, the interviewers smiled, nodded, and took lots of notes.

The night before his interview, John had envisioned the worst-case scenario. He imagined frowns, expressed disappointment, and being rejected right on the spot. But this interview was completely the opposite of all his fears. In fact, comparatively, he considered this interview process "a dream come true." He was sure he was perhaps the best candidate they had interviewed up to this point. At the end of the one hour scheduled interview, they asked John if he had any questions. Since it seemed they had answered most of his questions throughout their conversation, John just smiled and said, "I think you have answered all of the questions I have at this point – thank you."

They all stood and exchanged handshakes and niceties. One interviewer even encouraged John to enjoy the weather by going canoeing, one of the many hobbies John shared with them when they asked him to tell them about himself. This was one of the most enjoyable and positive experiences he had ever had in the interview process. John smiled, thanked them, and left the conference room walking on cloud nine.

Three weeks later, John was getting antsy. He had a couple of interviews in the interim but none that were nearly as pleasant and positive as this one. After all, this was the job he really wanted! Strangely, though, he had not heard a single word from the company. He sent his follow up email to the interviewers and even sent two additional emails to the Human Resources representative asking when he should expect to hear back from them. Still no word. With three weeks having past since the interview, John decided to make a call to the company to see if he could receive a status update on the position. The receptionist answered the phone and when John explained the purpose for his call, she forwarded him to the Human Resources department. The HR representative that answered the phone was very friendly and she gave an enthusiastic, "Hello!" When John enquired about the role, she apologized for the delay as several candidates had been calling. She said, "We want to thank you for your time. The interview panel felt that you did a nice job in the interview. However, they had someone else that they felt was a little more applicable for the role and that person has since been offered and accepted the position." She cordially said, "Thank you" and added, "You should be proud, you were in the top three candidates for this position."

When John hung up the phone, he was in absolute shock! He was sad, mad, frustrated, and then simply outraged. His head was spinning. How could this have happened? He really wanted this job and he felt as though he had created a strong connection with the interviewers who seemed to like his every response. How could they not, at the very least, invite him back for a second interview? Even though he was upset, John still found it within himself to muster up some self-coaching and find the bright spot in this circumstance. "The HR representative did say I was a strong candidate," he told himself. "Perhaps it just simply was not meant to be," he reasoned. "They do not know what they are missing and I know the right role will come my way, you watch and see." He convinced himself that he had done everything he could. After all, if the HR representative felt that he did well in the interview (top three), then there was no need to make any adjustments to his interviewing approach.

That night, John began preparing for the interview he had scheduled for the following morning. He stayed up for hours doing a Google search on the organization, reviewing the responsibilities of the job and writing down a few questions that he wanted to ask. He made extra copies of his resume, which were printed on expensive parchment paper, and set out his leather folder, nice pen, and blank paper pad for taking notes. He pressed his suit and polished his shoes. He was certain that tomorrow's interview experience would be better.

John's experience in the interview process is not unlike many of the clients that I work with. They feel as though they have done "all the right things" to prepare for the interview. They feel as though they have "nailed it," only to never hear from their interviewers again. It is a humbling reality that many have experienced at some time in their career. The things that John did to prepare for his interview were, for the most part, all good things to do. The problem is they are exactly what EVERYONE ELSE does too!

At one time, these steps were considered the best practices for interview preparation. However, technology has leveled the playing field. *Everyone* can access information from virtually anywhere and all candidates are Googling the company for facts and figures. *Everyone* is reviewing the job description in advance. While each of these things is necessary for success in the interview, it is not what will separate you from every other equally qualified candidate. The truth is, unless you change your approach, you will continue to get the same outcome. In other words, if you expect to land that dream job, you have to develop a more effective interviewing approach.

Albert Einstein is most famous for his equation, $E=MC^2$. However, one of his most profound theories was his definition of insanity, which I have written into a formula that looks something like this:

$$I = ST\infty EDR^X$$

This formula stands for: "Insanity (I) = Doing the Same Thing (ST) over and over again (∞) and Expecting Different Results (EDR), but never getting them (x)."

(Albert Einstein. Image credit: Library of Congress)

Yet we do this all the time in the interview process. People often interview, fail to get the job offer, and then immediately go to their next job interview utilizing the same steps and process that they did for their last interview (even though it was not successful).

Research surrounding communication was completed by Dr. Abraham Mehrebian in 1968 and has been reinforced countless times since. His research indicated that only 7% of our total communication is WHAT we say (our words). 93% of our total communication is HOW we say it (55% non-verbals & 38% vocal tone). Our non-verbal cues and vocal tone are far more impactful than the actual words we say. Make no mistake, words are important, even critical. However, the way in which we say them often supersedes the value of the words.

It is imperative that a candidate be fully aware of their non-verbals and their vocal tone during the interview.

Herein lies the challenge: Consider the average candidate preparing for an interview. 95% of the prep work is on the wording of their resume and on WHAT they plan to say during the interview. Very little time, if any, is spent on HOW they plan to communicate those things in the interview. Few candidates spend time thinking about HOW they are going to say what they need to say, the confidence they need to convey when asked about their strengths and weaknesses, the facial expressions they should use when asked a question for which they have no clear answer, and so on.

As an example, the interviewer asks a candidate, "Are you someone that is always prepared and, if so, give an example." The candidate pauses, uses verbal fillers such as "uh" & "um," as their eyes shift to the left or right in a desperate attempt to find a suitable response. All of this takes place in the span of only five to seven seconds and the candidate does not realize that they have already provided their "answer" (by the way they struggled to answer the question, their non-verbals gave them away and regardless of what words they choose to say, they appear non-verbally to be unprepared). Before the candidate provided their "answer," the interviewer had all the information they needed. They can see from this person's behavior that they were not prepared for this answer. Without speaking a word, the candidate's behavior (stall, eyes shifting, etc.) betrayed their words as they muttered nervously, "Sure, I'm always, uh, you know, prepared for anything." Judgments like this made by interviewers in these moments are often instantaneous and subconscious. Sometimes they are able to note those innuendoes and articulate their reasons for not hiring you for the job. However, most of the time, they simply get a bad *gut feeling* about the candidate and leave the interview saying, "I get the sense that this candidate is not the right 'fit' for the job."

Behavioral-Based Interviewing is the most common approach that top employers use today to interview and ultimately select candidates for open positions. Interviewers today rely heavily on the power and importance of behavioral-based interviewing. Most people who have heard of behavioral-based interviewing often believe that it is primarily about asking the candidate questions regarding what they *have done* in the past, such as, "In your previous roles, when have you managed people that did not perform up to par and what you *did* to resolve it?" Instead of asking a hypothetical question regarding what the candidate *might do* in a given scenario, behavioral-based interviewers want to hear about their actual on the job experience and what they *have done* vs. what they *might do*. While these types of "experience-based" questions are a key part of the behavioral-based interviewing process, behavioral-based interviewing is much more and often entails analyzing the candidate's physical behavior in the interview. Interviewers notice how you stand, the way you sit, the physical and facial gestures you use, how you pause, and the way in which you answer questions.

Behavioral-based interviewing is much more than simply asking you questions about what you have done and evaluating the words you speak to determine if you are a viable candidate. True behavioral-based interviewing goes well beyond the questions that the interviewer asks and focuses more on how the candidate is "behaving" during the conversation. Interviewers take mental notes on whether the candidate is confident, clear, articulate, self-assured, prepared, smooth, strong, warm, inviting, engaging, etc. Based off these interpersonal cues, the evaluation is made and the selection is determined for the candidate they feel is the best overall "fit" for the role, department, and/or organization.

Behavioral-Based Interviewing is so prevalent in the world of interviewing today that it is important to provide you with some tools and techniques that will help you to perform at your peak. If 93% of your communication in the interview is not the words you speak, it is imperative for us to address these issues clearly as we move forward. However, before we go into detail regarding these components, it is important for you to understand the challenges being faced by your future employers and how to think like the interviewer.

THINK LIKE THE INTERVIEWER

O ne of the first challenges that an applicant must overcome is their tendency to think like an applicant. In other words, most people get caught up into thinking like a candidate for the position and begin worrying about WHAT they should say. However, applicants often find it incredibly insightful to gain greater understanding of how the interviewer thinks. So, how does an interviewer/recruiter think?

Interviewers and recruiters are not always impressed with a resume that reads like a job description, which simply lists the key responsibilities of the job. For example,

- "Managed the Company Cost Cutting Team to discuss key concepts that support the organization's budget cutting strategies."

Yawn. Sigh. Hand me the next resume, please. Yet almost every resume we receive for review reads more like a boring, outdated job description with line after line of content that is lifeless and dull. Candidates often spend hour-upon-hour pouring over their resume to ensure each word is spelled correctly and every bullet is placed perfectly. While that is all well and good, it is not what piques the interest of the interviewer or recruiter. Yes, those things add value. Just not nearly the kind of value most people assign to them. Spending a large percent of your effort ensuring spelling and grammar are correct is a HUGE mistake. The very first thing our consulting firm does when asked by a client to help them enhance their resume is circle every single place on the resume (and there are usually 20 or more) where a number can be added to the content. That's right, a number. A statistic, a percentage, a dollar figure – any form of a number. Why? Because numbers transform a resume from a "job description" to a "performance highlight." Numbers transform a resume from a repository of past and present job responsibilities (tasks) into a hot sheet of your greatest accomplishments packed with numbers that represent what you have achieved.

Resumes are most effective when they highlight not what job responsibilities you have held in the past but <u>what results you have actually achieved</u>!

By adding numbers, the sample bullet I mentioned earlier in this section would be transformed from:

- "Managed the Company Cost Cutting Team to discuss key concepts that support the organization's budget cutting strategies."

<u>To</u>:

- "Managed the 'Company Cost Cutting' team consisting of seven Vice Presidents and four Directors to discuss the top five concepts to support the organization's budget cutting strategies resulting in in an annual savings of over $1.4 million dollars."

From 'flat' to 'stat' in seven seconds sharp! The resume is a "numbers game," both literally AND figuratively. Remember that interviewers care less about what you have *"done"* and care more about what you have *"achieved."* Adding stats and data to your resume makes all the difference in the world. This concept, alone, will add more value to your resume and your interviewing experience than you ever imagined. By spending the time to add these numbers to your resume, you are also effectively preparing key examples and important stats that will assist you during the interview.

Candidates will also benefit from further understanding how resumes are received by organizations, especially given the nearly exclusive use of technology today. Most organizations use electronic filters to automatically screen out resumes. Sophisticated word searches and phrase analysis software does the work that HR personnel use to do manually years ago. Resumes that pass the electronic filter are further reviewed to determine which applicants should receive a phone screen and/or a face-to-face interview.

First, let's discuss the dreaded electronic filter! When an application is submitted for a position, whether directly through their company's own on-line application procedures or via job search sites such as Monster.com, those resumes are pushed through a rigorous filter of key words and catch phrases that the recruiter or hiring manager has identified as critical for the position. The filters can be set for anything that ranges from a single word (i.e. marketing) to a couple of words stringed together (i.e. Masters Degree) to an entire phrase (i.e. manages multiple projects). Gone are the days when companies would physically receive over one hundred resumes in the mail and process each resume by hand. Now, electronic filters screen out a large percentage of the resumes that are submitted, sending an automatic email declining those candidates who failed to pass the initial filter. Today, the recruiter never lays eyes on the resumes that were filtered out.

Now imagine all the work you put into that beautifully crafted resume and it never being seen or read by the company you are applying to. Even more shocking to most candidates is the reality that half of the filtered out resumes may have included the best possible candidate for the position. However, because their resume was not set up to successfully pass the filter, it simply did not get reviewed by the recruiter or interviewer.

Candidates should customize every single resume they submit.

When it comes to customizing every resume being submitted, some candidates might say, "That is too much work and I like the way my resume looks." Did you catch that? They said, "too much work".

Remember what we shared earlier in this book. Some people spend twelve years getting through high school, then pay tens of thousand of dollars and over two thousand hours in study time, class time, and exams to get their Bachelor's degree (and still others spend even more money and another one thousand hours in study time, class time, and exams to get their Master's Degree), only to say that to tweak their resume for each job they apply for is "too much work". It is important to see the impact that a small adjustment to the resume can make for the positions you are applying for in the future.

I have good news. You do not have to change the entire resume for each position that you apply. Rather, you simply need to tweak it by ten percent and here is an easy way to do just that. Keep your resume ninety percent the same no matter where you apply. However, create a small section at the top of your resume entitled, "Key Qualifications". In this section, you simply include key words (preferably bullet points with only one to three words each) that describe you as a candidate (attributes, skills, characteristics, certifications, knowledge, etc.). You may select words and phrases such as "organized", "strong communicator", or "builds high-performance work teams".

The key here is that you customize this particular section of your resume by adding in key words and phrases from the job description of the role you are applying for or from an online position overview for the new role. Please note: only use the words from the job description that are true and honest about you (always tell the truth on your resume and in the interview). By adding these key words from the job description, you increase the likelihood of your resume passing through their initial electronic auto-filters and actually being reviewed by the recruiter/interviewer. Congratulations, you just made it through the electronic filter and someone may see your resume.

Next, once your resume passes through their initial auto-filters, a question that often arises is, *"How do I increase the likelihood that they will select me as a candidate to be phone screened/interviewed?"*

To increase your chances of being selected, you must understand that recruiters do not review resumes in order to *select* candidates into the interviewing pool, but to *reject* candidates from the interviewing pool. I spent many years of my career in recruiting and hiring. After hiring candidates at all levels of the organization and having to filter through endless resumes, I have found this to be true for me and for every single person that I have talked to in the profession. For example, when recruiters receive the resumes that pass their auto-filters, they may receive (depending on the size of the organization and the position that is posted) up to thirty, fifty, even one hundred or more resumes to review for this one position alone. Note, however, that recruiters/human resources professionals often have many open positions so they receive this many resumes for each of their open roles. Due to their heavy workload and the fact that their key performance measure is "how long it takes to fill each position", the recruiter simply does not have time to personally and carefully read every single resume. They have to find a way to quickly get through countless resumes.

As a result, they must establish a process by which they will peruse through the resumes and pull out the top candidates to phone screen/interview. Most professionals that have been in the industry for many years report that they can quickly (within ten seconds or less) spot something missing, inaccurate, strange, confusing, or boring about a resume so it is often easier to quickly establish a "no" pile before pairing them down to a highly qualified top ten or fifteen resumes that are placed into the "yes" pile. These resumes are the ones that are read carefully to determine which candidates they will phone screen and ultimately bring into the company for face-to-face interviews.

What does all this mean? It means that when you think like a recruiter/interviewer, resumes are not designed (in the real world) to select candidates "in" but to select candidates "out." That means you want to ensure that your resume is constructed appropriately, effectively, and accurately. It also means you have only ten seconds to impress upon the recruiter that your resume is not a "toss pile" resume. One very effective way to accomplish this is to bold one bullet point from each role you have reflected on your resume. The bullet point you will want to select is the one that most closely reflects characteristics listed in the job description of the position for which you are applying. It is important that only one bullet from each position overview on your resume is placed in bold font. When everything is highlighted on your resume as "important," nothing appears to be important. The key here is that the bullets you place in bold font will draw the eyes of the recruiter/interviewer to your most relevant achievements that apply most to the new role for which you are applying. This, in turn, will cause the recruiter/interviewer to more likely place your resume on the initial keep pile. It is a simple yet very practical and extremely effective strategy to use when developing your resume.

It is also important to understand the daily work reality of a recruiter/ interviewer. First, the recruiter is often contacted by the hiring manager who expresses the need to fill a position. Then, these two individuals often spend a considerable amount of time discussing the desired characteristics that the hiring manager is looking for in the candidates, the minimum skill requirements needed for the position, and a general experience profile of the ideal candidate.

Recruiters frequently find themselves having conversations with key leaders and hiring managers who become frustrated when the recruiter sends them candidates who were not truly qualified for the position. As a result, the recruiter is constantly honing their own phone screening and face-to-face interviewing skills to ensure they can assess candidates quickly, effectively, and accurately.

Additionally, the recruiter is often being reminded by their own manager that they are being measured by how quickly they fill each position. Therefore, a recruiter that makes the decision to give you an interview has a vested interest in your success. Secretly, they are cheering for you to nail the job interview and silently hoping the hiring manager likes you. That makes them, as a recruiter, look brilliant! On the other hand, if for any reason the interview panel does not like you as a candidate, then the recruiter looks ineffective in their role. This is important to note because candidates often feel a great deal of pressure if they have not heard from the recruiter in two to three days (or sometimes in two to three hours). If the recruiter liked you as a candidate enough to bring you into the organization to interview you for a position, then they are secretly cheering you on. That is because if your interview does not go well, the recruiter will have to address the inevitable questions that are often asked by the interviewing panel members after a poor interview: *"Why did you bring*

THEM in for an interview? Are you sure you know how to do your job? This candidate was not even close to what we were looking for."

This is why the recruiter wants to do everything they can to help you get the job. Doing so will improve their "time to fill" quota and will impress the hiring manager. Doing so results in greater job security, potentially higher salary, and the greater likelihood of an end-of-year bonus. Trust me, having spent years in the recruiting and hiring arena, recruiters want you to get the job. In fact, they <u>need</u> you to get the job. And they will do everything possible to ensure you are successful in the interviewing process. Why? Because:

Finding Someone the Hiring Manager Likes Enough to Offer the Position = The Recruiter Looks Brilliant. Period.

PREPARATION IS POWER

———∾∾∾———

S uccessfully navigating an interview consists of several important factors, none of which are more important than the power of proper
preparation. However, it's not just important that candidates prepare
for the interview, but that they prepare properly and effectively for the
interview. Most people believe that properly preparing for an interview
includes activities such as purchasing a new suit, remembering to provide
a firm handshake, practicing looking the interviewer in the eye, being sure
to use the interviewer's name, thinking through the possible questions that
might arise during their interview, searching the Internet for facts about
the company, and the list goes on. All of these things are important and I
encourage all candidates to do each and every one. All of these things are
important, necessary, and critical to success. However, these things are
only the basic components of proper preparation. If you really want to nail
the interview and impress your interviewers, then you must avoid the top
two "preparation pitfalls" and be sure to practice the "preparation power
play" that positively separates you from all other candidates.

PREPARATION PITFALL #1:
Nothing Written, Nothing Prepared.

One of the consistent patterns we see with candidates is that they typically go into their interviews with only a few copies of their resume, a leather padfolio with blank paper, and a pen. One challenge with this approach is that when the candidate opens their padfolio at the start of the interview to take notes, the interviewers immediately notice that there is absolutely nothing written on the paper in front of them. Because they have no other physical evidence to judge you by, the interviewer makes an automatic assumption (fair or unfair) that this candidate came to the interview unprepared.

I routinely share the following simple fact with candidates on a regular basis: *"The physical universe does not lie."* The best indication an interviewer has to determine how you will perform in the future, if hired, is how you are performing during their interview right now. Regardless of whether that is fair or unfair, right or wrong, good or bad, the one thing we do know for sure is that it is a reality.

The simple truth is that interviewers can only go by how you are acting and speaking in the moment. There is no documentary on your past performance nor any way to see into your future. Therefore, the only information they have to predict how you will perform for their organization in the future is how you are performing during the one hour (sometimes more or less) interview you have with them in this moment. As a result, when they see that you have nothing written on the blank note pad in front of you, they have to assume that you will also go into your first meeting as a company employee with nothing prepared.

PREPARATION PITFALL #2:
HandWritten Notes Get You Nowhere.

Some candidates kick it up a notch by adding handwritten notes to their arsenal of materials prepared for the interview. They may write out a few questions in advance on their padfolio and reference them when needed in the interview. At least the pages in front of them are not blank, which is a plus. However, they do not realize that this also conveys a clear message to the interviewer. Most candidates may not be aware that this is sending a negative, subconscious message to the people that may be holding the power to their next career opportunity in their hands. When a candidate enters the interview with a padfolio containing a half-page of handwritten notes, most interviewers make an instantaneous assumption as to when those notes were written. I have interviewed countless professionals who interview candidates on a regular basis and I ask them when they believe the candidate wrote the handwritten notes they see in their padfolio. With very few exceptions, the vast majority tell me that they believe the candidate's notes were most likely written in the lobby as they waited for the interview to begin. These highly talented professionals interview candidate after candidate and are well attuned to every nuance of each applicant. Regardless of whether it is accurate or not, fair or unfair, they make an automatic assumption as to when those notes were prepared. And the assumption is, almost always, "moments before the interview began."

When a candidate has a few handwritten notes on the page, they can not help but assume that the notes were written a few minutes prior to the interview (most likely at breakfast that morning or in the lobby before you were called into the interview). Because the interviewers have nothing else on which to predict your future performance, they have to assume that you will enter your first important meeting at their organization in the same manner: a sheet of paper with a few handwritten notes that were created minutes before walking through the door. As a result, they may assume you are not as organized and committed as you might state you are during the interview. As mentioned in the chapter entitled *Behavioral-Based Interviewing*, interviewers today focus on the power of interpreting your behavior to fill in the missing pieces of the puzzle that your words may not fully indicate. This means that when you enter a room with no notes or simply a few handwritten notes, the interviewers have no other option but to believe that this will be how you will "behave" on the job. In other words, they interpret through this behavior that you are generally someone who is unprepared, regardless of all the words you use in the interview to describe how incredibly prepared you are for any situation.

Through my personal research, I have also noticed that many candidates never open their padfolio during the interview, which is a huge mistake. Candidates frequently tell me that they believe it makes them look more professional to speak "off the cuff." Nothing could be further from the truth. Rather than appear more professional when speaking "off the cuff," the candidate often appears to be more unprepared, as though they are making up their answers as they go.

PREPARATION POWER PLAY:
A Typed Interview Prep Sheet

The third and final approach that candidates utilize when preparing for an interview includes a major upgrade from handwritten notes, which is a one-page typed document containing one-word bullet points that reference key information for the interview.

If you have ever attempted any of the first two approaches to preparing for an interview, you are not alone. The first two approaches I described above (no notes or handwritten notes in preparation for the interview) are the most common approaches that millions of candidates use on a daily basis. Let me describe what I have found to be a "preparation power play" in the interview process.

I am a big believer in the philosophy that "less is more." The most effective component that I have witnessed candidates use to prepare for an interview is the creation of a single sheet of typed bullet points that include some of the key elements they want to share during their interview. These components should include the following:

- Key accomplishments you want to be sure to share
- Three things you will use to tell them about yourself
- Three strengths
- Two weaknesses
- Your greatest success
- A time when you failed
- Five questions you want to ask the interviewer
- Your final closing question of the interview

I call this document the "Interview Prep Sheet." This single sheet of typed paper, along with your padfolio and several copies of your resume, is all you will need to take into the interview. Many candidates ask me the question, *"Does this really need to be typewritten?"* The answer, in short, is absolutely yes. Here is why.

This typed interview prep sheet is helpful for your reference during the interview. It will help you in advance of the interview to think through key questions that will be asked throughout the process, stay focused on important facts, and support you when challenging questions arise.

However, it is important for you to understand that while this document will *help* you, it is not *for* you. It is for the interviewer. The power behind this simple gesture of typing this basic information in preparation for your interview is that it demonstrates to the interviewer that you are someone who truly is organized and prepared. Their assumption is that you have put a lot of thought into this interview and that you have really done your homework.

After researching and interviewing recruiters and professionals who interview candidates on a regular basis, their automatic assumption (good or bad, fair or unfair) is that a candidate who brings a typed document to their interview has really put a lot of thought in this position and that the candidate has really done their homework. Their automatic assumption is that you are both organized and well prepared. If you are this prepared for an interview, their conclusion is that when you come into their meeting on your first day on the job, you will also be this organized and prepared at work. Even though the interview prep sheet will be helpful for you to reference during the interview, it is ultimately designed to make a clear statement to the interviewer about your interest in the role and your professional approach to the job.

I highly recommend that you avoid the preparation pitfalls and the first two approaches described (no notes or simply handwritten notes). They are deadly interview traps and many candidates have fallen into them. Instead, use the "preparation power play" and you will find that this strategy will have a huge positive impact on the outcome of your interview.

The "Interview Prep Sheet" has been included below and the following chapters will help you to effectively prepare your answers to each section of this document.

Nailed It!: Ten Keys to Crushing the Interview©: Interview Prep Sheet

Name: _____

Keys
-
-
-
-

Frame
-
-
-

Strengths
-
-
-

Weaknesses
-
-

Success
- (recent/relevant)

Failure
- (learned)

Questions
-
-
-

Closing
- Most Confidence, Might be Applicable

Give not Get, Alignment, Short-Long-Short, Have Done not Will Do

Key #1: Frame It Up

The most frequently asked question in the interview process is "Tell me about yourself." According to an article in classesandcareers. org dated October 2011 and reinforced by several researchers many times since, this question continues to be the most popular question in the interview process today.

"Tell me about yourself" is the #1 most common interview question

From an interviewing perspective, this particular question is the most fascinating to me. Few candidates know the "perfect" answer to this question, primarily because no one actually spends time thinking about how they would answer this particular question. After working with thousands of clients in the area of advanced interviewing, not a single person could actually state that they had a well thought out, written plan for how they would answer this question. In fact, I have discovered that almost every single candidate feels no need to actually *prepare* an answer to this question. Their reasoning is, "*who knows me better than I do?*" As a result, they are overly confident that when the time comes, they will easily be able to pull off an answer to this question.

Rather than spend any time preparing for this question, candidates spend what little time they use to prep for the interview on what they believe to be more "serious & challenging" questions like *"What are your weaknesses?"* or *"Why do you want this position?"* However, my research shows that over and over again, this question is, without exception, the most *botched* interview question at all professional levels. There are several reasons why this is true.

The most commonly <u>botched</u> interview question is "Tell me about yourself"

First, we have to understand that this is typically the very first question asked in almost every single interview. Why is this the case? Realistically, interviewers all over the globe could ask this question at any point of the interview and it would be considered "fair" placement for this question. They do not, however, ask this question anywhere else in the interview than at the very beginning and there is a perfectly good reason for it. Interviewers ask this question at the beginning of the interview <u>*not*</u> because they stayed up late the night before the interview and wrestled with where they should best place this question. Interviewers ask this question at the beginning of the interview <u>*not*</u> because the Human Resources representative *strategically* placed this question at the top of the interview guide that they put together to support the interviewers in their efforts to select the right candidate. In fact, for organizations that have taken the time to put together a well thought out and carefully crafted interview guide, 95% of them never even include this question on the interview guide.

Why, then, do nearly 99% of interviewers ask this question at the very beginning of the interview? The answer is simple and is a powerful key to nailing your next interview. Interviewers ask this question prior to asking their formal interview questions because they do not see it as an actual interview question. Almost without exception, most interviewers ask this question at the beginning of the interview because they see it as a "warm up" or "ice breaker" to the interview. For most interviewers, this question is seen much like the question *"Nice weather we are having today, isn't it?"* or *"did you have any difficulty finding the building?"* The give-away is how the question is typically framed, such as, *"So, before we <u>start</u> the interview, tell me a little bit about yourself."* This is very important for you to note. Often the "tell me about yourself" question is coupled with the phrase "before we get started." Most interviewers ask this question in an impromptu manner and initiate the formal interview with this informal question thinking it will be a nice way to get the dialogue "off the ground." I call it "the non-question." And that is just one of the complexities that this question offers a candidate.

The second reason candidates typically *botch* the "tell me about yourself" question is that they do not understand the interviewers perspective on this question in the first place. In fact, I realized that if I am going to help candidates absolutely nail the job interview, I *must first* help them understand the interviewers' perspective on this question.

I have asked hundreds of interviewers in-depth questions to understand their perspective on why they ask this opening "request for information." I was absolutely stunned to hear their candid responses. Not only do most *interviewers not* understand that this question is, at its core, a "non-question," but they, themselves, do not actually know what they want to hear when they ask it. Let me explain further.

When I asked hundreds of interviewers, *"What is it that you are looking for when you ask the 'Tell me about yourself' question?"* they each required a few moments to consider their answer. What that means in lay terms is that they do not actually know what they are looking for in the answer to this question. As a result, they do not have a formal "right answer" that they are looking for. However, given a few minutes to think about it, they could write it down and give a logical, professional answer. By the way, it took many interviewers several moments to figure out what exactly *it is* that they are looking for when they ask candidates this question. Even for those who interview candidates daily in their careers, they did not have an immediate planned response. Most interviewers were willing to say, *"I don't have a formal [written or pre-thought out] answer I'm looking for when I ask this question–I'll just know it when I hear it."* Interviewers simply do not have a clear idea that rolls off their tongue as to what the "magic words" are that they want to hear when they ask you the question *"Tell me about yourself."*

For this reason, the absolute <u>worst</u> answer a candidate can give in response to this question is, *"What do you want to hear?"* Not only is it a poor answer (because it makes the candidate appear unprepared), it also make the candidate appear that they are willing to just simply feed back the answers to the interviewer what the interviewer wants to hear. Worse yet is the fact that by asking *"what do you want to hear,?"* the candidate is now interviewing the interviewer and putting them on the spot. Because the interviewer does not have a preconceived notion of what they want to hear when they ask this question, they have to mentally scramble their brain for a moment to come up with a quick answer that sounds polished and professional.

Know this; interviewers are professionals and when "put on the spot," they can provide an answer as to what they want to hear when asking candidates this question. Without even realizing it, though, candidates are actually putting the interviewer "on the spot" and the interviewer feels the pressure to come up with the "right answer." Their typical response sounds something like, *"Oh, you know, things like your background, maybe where you are from, relevant experience, perhaps something about your edu-cation, that kind of thing."* Almost every time their answers are not suc-cinct and clear because they had not honestly thought about what they wanted to hear from the candidate on <u>*this*</u> particular question in advance of the interview.

Also important to note is the fact that it often irritates interviewers that the very first question they ask you is being turned back to them with a request for them to explain themselves. Do not get me wrong, there are moments in an interview where it is effective, even encouraged, to momentarily take control of the interview and to ask a question of the interviewer. However, the very beginning of the interview *is not* where you want to do this. Why? Because a critical reason as to why candidates *"botch"* this interview questions is due to the following known statistic.

Hiring decisions are made within the first ninety seconds!

In a study of over 2,000 bosses per the Classesandcareers.com article dated October 2011, thirty three percent claimed they knew within the first 90 seconds of the interview whether or not they would hire a can-didate. When candidates choose to answer the very first question of the interview <u>*with*</u> a question (*"What would you like to hear?"*), I call it the "death rattle." You may have heard the old expression, "you don't have a second chance to make a good first impression." Visual and vocal impres-sions are made within the first thirty seconds of an encounter; therefore, a candidate's first impressions are made at the very beginning of the inter-view with their answer to ***this*** question. Remember, the interviewer does not even see this as one of their actual interview questions. So, you have not even technically started the interview and the whole thing can be completely *"botched"* before the interviewer even asks their first formal interview question.

Every interviewer is looking for something different when they ask the question, "Tell me about yourself"

The third reason candidates completely *botch* the "tell me about yourself" interview question is that almost every interviewer is looking for something <u>different</u> in what they would call their *ideal* response. My research with interviewers on this topic has revealed that there is no concrete pattern for what interviewers are looking for as the best right answer.

In one point in my research, I was in a conference room at a university discussing this topic with eighteen seasoned masters degree graduates and asked them to privately write down what things they would like to hear in response to the question, *"Tell me about yourself."* I then asked them to share with the other participants in the room, one-at-a time, exactly what they had written down. Remarkably, almost every interviewer had written something completely different from every other interviewer in the room. Sure, there were some similarities; but for the most part, each list they generated was in some form different from the other participants in the room. We charted their answers on a flip chart and even they were astonished at the varying degree of responses in the room. When asked what they were looking for in the answer to the question "Tell me about yourself," all eighteen interviewers (interviewing for the exact same position) articulated something completely different than their professional counterparts. One interviewer shared, *"I want to hear one thing and one thing only — the reason I should hire you for the role."* Another interviewer stated shyly, *"I just want to hear what their passions and hobbies are ... that's how I get to know them personally."* Yet a third interviewer boldly stated,

"I don't care about any of those things—the only thing I want to know is their relevant job experience to see if they are a possible fit for this job." A fourth interviewer declared, *"I just want to see how they engage me and the other interviewing panel members, which will tell me whether or not they are a people person and how they would fit into our current company culture."*

Since then, I have performed this exercise with countless professionals at all organizational levels and the results are always the same. Candidate after candidate approaches this question thinking, *"I will wing it and, because I am a professional who happens to also be a pretty good communicator, I will be able to pull it off."* However, most people *botch* this question terribly and do not even realize it. In fact, through my research with interviewing panel members, most candidates who completely *botch* this question have no idea that they have done so. How does that happen? The answer is simple. The average candidate spends less than thirty minutes preparing for an interview and rarely gives this question any thought. When the question is finally asked, with no planned response they begin to talk. Some keep on talking. Some keep on talking for a really long time. They do not know what the interviewer is looking for (and, as mentioned, neither does the interviewer) so they just start sharing "stuff" and hope something hits the mark.

The two most common challenges that interviewers tell me they experience are, 1) Candidates say too little. For example, they might say, "I'm from a small town, I went to XYZ State University and majored in Communications, and I like listening to music;" or, 2). Candidates most often say too much. For example, *"I come from a large family of seven kids, I'm the youngest, we were a close knit family and still enjoy spending time together. We had a family reunion last month and tons of people showed up; it was a blast. I went to ABC University to get my Bachelor's degree, I love learning, I met my wife there and we dated for six years before getting married, and my family is very supportive of my career goals. We like to go to movies and we will some times stay seated after the movie is over and just talk and talk and laugh about lines from the movie. We went to 59 different movies last year and we will go to 4 movies this coming weekend. It is our favorite and...and....and...*" [first breath], then continue speaking, etc., etc., etc.).

My research unveiled the fact that the average answer to this question is three-and-a-half minutes in length. At first glance, three-and-a-half minutes does not sound that long. However, if I were to force you to listen to music on a static-filled radio station, you would likely be shocked at how long three-and-a-half minutes can be! I use that analogy because many interviewers articulate a lengthy answer to this non-question "Tell me about yourself" sounding just like a staticky radio station. They are willing to listen for about thirty seconds in hopes that the static will give way to a clear and relevant answer. However, if you do not answer this question succinctly with what they are hoping to hear, the static becomes overwhelming and they begin to tune you out.

I always encourage candidates to respond to this question in thirty to forty-five seconds. That means that if the average person is talking for three-and-a-half minutes, the interviewer has *tuned out* nearly 80% of everything they shared. Keep in mind that these are professional interviewers who will not hold up their hands and say, *"Whoa! Okay, that is WAY too long of an answer and I am now bored. Can you PLEASE stop talking now?!"* Rather, as professionals, the interviewers will look at you and nod their heads and even smile as you ramble on for 210 seconds. Most candidates share with me that following their interview, they felt the interview went well because the interviewer "seemed interested" in what they had to say based on their positive smiles and head nods. Most interviewers make great eye contact, smile, and nod their heads as you speak.

The interviewer never tells the candidate that they just *botched* the very first question, leaving a very poor first impression and setting an ineffective tone for the rest of the interview. Rather, they smile and nod their head all the while their eyes glaze over as their minds drift to a less staticky radio station in their brain.

The good news is the fact that there is a way to answer this question in thirty to forty-five seconds that makes a great first impression and establishes a professional tone for the rest of the interview. Let me reiterate this point:

The key to nailing the first 90 seconds of the interview is to effectively Frame Up your answer to the question "Tell me about yourself"

Opening the interview with a powerful answer to this first "non-question" is your first and most crucial opportunity for a critical win that will separate you from all other candidates.

Now that you know that almost all interviewers are not consciously aware of what they are looking for in the "right" answer to this question, let me show you how to "frame up" your response. To frame up your response, you will utilize only three key components placed in a logical, linear fashion and then ask the interviewer if this information is adequate to answer their question. The process looks something like this:

Interviewer: *"Tell me a little bit about yourself"*
Candidate: *"Absolutely. Why don't I first share with you my educational background, tell you about my two most relevant positions to this role, and share a key characteristic that I bring to the table when it comes to this particular position. How does that sound to you?"*

The frame up for this question should always incorporate only three simple components (more than three and it becomes too difficult to follow). However, please note that each person may have their own unique frame up for this question. For some candidates, education would be ideal to share in the interview. For others, education is not their strong point so they would not utilize education in their framing. Rather, that candidate may choose to explain trainings or certifications they have completed over the years. For many candidates, relevant roles to this job are often very helpful and valuable to include in the framing. For other candidates, they may instead choose to share a key project or initiative that they were responsible for as well as the successful outcome of that project. The key is that the frame up consists of only three elements that will help the candidate keep their answer brief and succinct.

I do encourage for the third component of the frame up, however, that candidates end their frame up with a key characteristic about themselves that is relevant and necessary in the new role for which they are applying. First, the interviewer will get to hear you state a true characteristic about yourself in your own words that is relevant to this role. Additionally, stating a key characteristic about yourself allows you to move to your first question that we encourage in the interview, which I'll cover in the next few paragraphs.

Sample Frame Up Includes:

- My Education (alternative might be trainings or certifications)
- Most Relevant Experience (alternative might be a project/ initiative)
- Key Characteristic (that is true & matches the new job description)

First, by framing up the answer in this fashion, it makes logical sense to the interviewer and you have done all the hard work for them by building an outline for them to easily follow. Because most interviewers have not truly pre-determined what they really want to hear when asking you this question, it is refreshing for them to receive a clear answer provided in a logical fashion.

Last, by asking the interviewer if the outline you provided for them is adequate, you give them the opportunity and authority to accept your proposal. My personal research revealed that over 95% of interviewers not only accepted the proposed frame up, they also were impressed that the candidate was able to navigate this question with such ease and command. This is a great advantage for you and immediately begins to separate you from all other equally qualified candidates. Your professional, well-planned frame-up will set you apart from other candidates and distinguish you as both organized and articulate. Interviews are stressful. When you clearly plan and know how you are going to answer the very first interview question, it gives you greater confidence to manage the rest of the interview.

There may be times when the interviewer states, *"I'd also like to hear about your personal interests and hobbies."* Me research indicates that less than five percent of interviewers ask for additional information. If and when this occurs, however, you simply agree to provide the information and incorporate it appropriately into your already developed frame work for answering this question.

The answer to "Tell me about yourself" should always be answered with information that is <u>Relevant</u> to the new role.

Candidates sometimes want to include more personal information in their answer to this question so as to allow the interviewer to get to know them on a personal basis. My recommendation, however, is to always answer this question with relevant information that is applicable to performing well in the new role. Only include personal information (i.e. "I have a wife, two kids, we like theatre productions, and we like going to Fall festivals each year") when the interviewer specifically requests it. Candidates are often tempted to share too much personal information. My recommendation, however, is to always keep your answers professional and work-related. There are two reasons for this. First, if the interviewer is not an individual who typically likes to hear this kind of information in the interview, it can cause you to appear unfocused and your personal interests irrelevant to the role. As a result, you could leave a poor first impression within the first few minutes of the interview and not even realize it. Secondly, because of the impromptu, unorganized nature of sharing personal information, it is easy for the candidate to get "off topic" and begin to ramble.

Once you have created a clear and succinct frame-up for this question, it will be critical that your answer be between thirty and forty-five seconds. Most candidates either ramble or share too little information. You, as an advanced interviewer, however, will follow your frame-up and answer all three components within your self-imposed thirty to forty-five second window. By doing so, you will often be the first (perhaps only) candidate to be extremely clear on your response to this critical first question, which takes place in the first 90 seconds of the interview. You will be sharing interesting and relevant information in a reasonable time frame and you will have left the interviewer with a very powerful and strong first impression. You want to finish your response within this timeframe so that it leaves them wanting to hear more not less.

Finally, it is time to segue in to the actual interview in a powerful way, To close this opening "non-question" in a powerful way, you will next roll immediately into your first question for the interviewer. You have framed up the answer to the "Tell me about yourself" question and followed the outline by answering this question within a thirty to forty-five second timeframe. You have also finished your frame up with a key characteristic. For example, *"I believe one characteristic that I bring to the table for this position is the ability to communicate well at all levels of the organization."* Now, without pause or hesitation, you will roll directly into your first question. The question you will ask following your frame up to the opening question is, *"That is one characteristic about me – however, I imagine that there are two or three key characteristics that you are looking for in the candidates for this position. What do you suppose those characteristics might be?"*

When asked comfortably and humbly, interviewers are often more willing to share their top two to three characteristics. These characteristics are critical as they reveal the "secrets" that will help you to win the rest of the interview.

It is important to note that you should not reply to any of these characteristics during and/or after the interviewer answers this question! In other words, they are revealing their "secrets" to help you succeed in the interview. For example, the interviewer may state, *"the characteristics we are looking for include strong communication skills, the ability to juggle multiple priorities, and experience managing large teams".* As a result, it feels too conniving if you reply with the statement, *"Great because I am a great communicator, I juggle multiple projects all the time, and I have managed lots of people!".* Rather, the only response or action I encourage you to take is a simple one. That action is to simply say, *"thank you."*

While it may seem a bit counter-intuitive, it is also important that you not write down what they are saying. While it is important for you to remember what they say, this is not the time to be writing it down. It is a time to be listening. Writing anything while they are being vulnerable and sharing their top characteristics they are looking for often feels uncomfortable for the interviewer and could cause them to feel *duped*. Simply maintain eye contact with them and allow them to begin asking their next standard interview question once they have finished their response. Say "thank you" and then pause and let them start with their first *formal* interview question.

You are now armed with the three key characteristics that the interviewer is looking for in top candidates for this role and you will want to strategically "sprinkle" them lightly into the answers to their forthcoming questions. Note: timing is everything. Typically I encourage candidates not to use one of these characteristics for at least two to three questions beyond that initial reveal. Further, I encourage them to allow for two or three questions between each time they refer to one of the shared key characteristics. Otherwise, once again, it may feel to the interviewer as though you are simply feeding them the answers they want to hear rather than speaking authentically from your heart from real actual experience.

Think of it this way. You ask a friend about their favorite cookie ingredient. Without hesitation, they respond, "Chocolate chips!" Armed with this new information, you eagerly whip up a batch of cookies and dump the entire five pound bag of chocolate chips into that one batch. Sure, your friend may like chocolate chips, but this may seem a little overwhelming for some people. However, with just the right amount of chocolate chips sprinkled into the mix, your friend is sure to enjoy the treat and the gesture. In the same way, when you lightly sprinkle into your answers how your skill and experience match the key characteristics that they are looking for in candidates, the results will not be overwhelming but rather refreshing. It will often feel like just the right mix. Allowing for the first ten to fifteen minute gap before you add that first ingredient means your answers will flow more smoothly and feel more genuine.

As is the case in every aspect of the interview, you must always be honest and always tell the truth. For example, if you truly only possess one of the three key attributes that the interviewer articulates as the three key characteristics that they are looking for in candidates for this role, then only *sprinkle* in that characteristic throughout your interview. Under no circumstance is it appropriate for candidates to be dishonest about a skill, characteristic or experience. It is not worth compromising your integrity in order to win the interview. The reality is that your honesty and integrity will shine brighter than any false information another candidate might offer. However, if you do happen to have all the characteristics that the interviewer reveals, it is incredibly advantageous to strategically sprinkle these characteristics into your answers over the course of your thirty-minute to one-hour interview and let them see that you are a perfect fit for the role.

Remember our chocolate chip cookies? We spread the chips evenly in the mix for the right results. Equally important is knowing that we do not have to use all the chips for every batch. It is appropriate to save some for another batch at another time. The same is true in interviewing. There is no need, or time, to share your entire life story, every instance of how you have employed your skill and experience, and every leadership highlight. Save some for the second, third or even fourth interview. Make the interviewer want to bring you back to find out more about your experience and you will walk away saying, *"I Nailed it!"* More importantly, so will your interviewers!

To bring this entire segment together, let me share with you what an effective answer to the question *"Tell me about yourself"* might look like from start to finish. This is simply an example of how best to answer this question. It will be important for you to personalize your answer given your own background and experiences. A sample answer to *"Tell me about yourself"* might sound like this:

Interviewer: *"Thanks for coming in today and I've been looking forward to our conversation. Before we begin the interview, why don't you tell me a little bit about yourself?"*

Candidate: *"Absolutely. Why don't I first tell you about my <u>education</u>. I'll then share with you some information about my <u>two most relevant roles</u> to this position. Last, I'll share with you what I think the <u>key characteristic</u> is that I bring to this position. How does that sound to you?"*

Interviewer: *"That sounds great."*

Candidate: *"I received my Bachelor's Degree in Interpersonal and Public Communication with a minor in Psychology from Bowling Green State University in Ohio. I then later received my Masters Degree in Executive Human Resource Development from Xavier University. My two most relevant roles to this position include the ten years I worked as an HR Leader at a multi-billion dollar global retailer working on several division-wide projects with team members that ranged from entry-level professionals to Sr. Executives. Most recently, I started my own consulting firm where I have provided executive coaching as well as professional training and development for senior level executives in fortune 100 companies. Last, the key characteristic that I bring to this position is the fact that I have the ability to communicate effectively with individuals at all levels of the organization, from entry-level professionals to CEO. And while that is just one key characteristic that I feel I bring to this role, I would imagine that there are three or four key characteristics that you are looking for in candidates for this position. What do you suppose those characteristics might be?"*

Interviewer: *"Great question. For this position, we really need someone who has experience working with large teams. We also need someone who can multi-task and juggle multiple priorities with ease. Last, we have to have someone who is organized and can achieve results quickly."*

Candidate: (Listening and making eye contact–Not writing notes in this moment). *"Thank You."* (Does not explain in this moment how they have all these key characteristics and will sprinkle in those answers slowly over the course of the interview).

Interviewer: *"So, lets get started. Can you tell me about ...."*

By starting off the interview in this fashion, you will have provided an incredible first impression! You will have been ready for the first question of the interview, framed up the questions in an orderly and logical fashion, and asked the question that will provide you with the keys to unlocking your opportunity to win over the interviewer. You achieved all of this within the first sixty to ninety seconds of the interview. Following the frame up model and approach, you will have effectively achieved what I call the "Five C's" of the Interview Process."

Frame Up Helps You to Achieve The Five C's of the Interview:

- Calm (You know what to say and you are at ease)
- Clear (You have answers that the interviewer can understand and follow)
- Concise (You complete your answer in thirty to forty-five seconds)
- Confident (You know what to say and you speak it with conviction)
- Connected." (You articulate how your experience applies to the role)

Congratulations! You just *Nailed* the first question of the interview. In the chapters that follow, we will explore and expand upon the other key questions that will comprise the remainder of your interview.

Now It Is Your Turn:

Below, create your frame-up for the first question of the interview. Determine what your first two components will be (education, relevant experience, key accomplishment, etc.). The third component should be a true key characteristic about yourself that would be very beneficial to have if you acquire the position for which you are interviewing. Then practice this verbiage as well as the first question that you will roll into following the description of yourself. Please note that the frame-up (especially the key characteristic) that you choose to share in your next interview may change from interview to interview depending on the position that you are applying for in the moment. As a result, you will want to update your frame-up in preparation for each new interview.

My Frame-Up *(Tell Me About Yourself)*

1st:_____

_____

_____

2nd:_____

_____

_____

3rd (key characteristic): _____

_____

Practice Rolling into your 1st Question: "That is one characteristic that I bring to this role. However, I imagine that there are three or four key characteristics that you are looking for in candidates for this position. What do you suppose those characteristics might be?"_____

_____

_____

KEY #2: GIVE NOT GET

⟶ ✿✿ ⟵

The question, "Why do you want this position?," is another commonly asked interview questions at all professional levels. Interviewers ask this question to understand the motivations and aspirations that drive candidates to apply and interview for a role. This is one of those questions for which candidates rarely seek an exceptional answer because they believe the standard answer sounds good enough. As a result, candidates who could easily set themselves apart as a top-tier candidate often fail to do so. The typical answer to this question often follows this pattern:

Interviewer: *"Why do you want this position?"*

Candidate: *"I want this position because this is a great company for me to work with and it will really help me to build my experience and skill set. I also feel that it will help me to gain the experience needed for me to go to the next level. I have always wanted to work with your company and I feel I can learn and grow from the leaders of this organization. Last, I like the products and services produced by this organization and I feel that I can benefit from my association with this company and the great things we do in the industry."*

At first glance, this answer may sound just *fine*, which is why it is a big part of the problem. The enemy of "great" is "good" and the enemy of "outstanding" is "great." Candidates share this type of answer to this question because they feel it is strong enough to keep them *in the running*. However, doing so is to miss a huge opportunity to truly stand out from all other candidates.

The problem with how nearly every candidate answers this question is that the answer itself is "I-centered" vs "company-centered." After interviewing and video recording countless candidates in preparation for their interview, it is very apparent that over 90%+ of candidates respond to this question in a similar fashion. So being more intentional about your response and understanding exactly how to shape this answer will catapult you to the top of the list of outstanding candidates.

If you look closely, the sample answer above is completely about the benefits that the candidate will receive if they are selected for the position. In fact, at its core, it is an extremely self-centered answer that is laced with "I want...," "...great company for me...," "....help me to build....", "...help me to gain...," "...I can learn...," and "...I can benefit..." just to name a few. Essentially, the candidate is letting the company know that from their perspective, "it is all about ME." Most people who utilize a similar answer to the one that I outlined above would never say that they felt their answer to the question was so self-centered. This is because they are looking at it from a candidate's perspective and not from the hiring manager's perspective. When I asked one candidate why they answered in this way, they quickly justified their answer by stating, *"You asked ME to tell you why I want this position so why would I not answer the question with how receiving this position will benefit ME?!?"*

This gave me such great insight into why it is so easy for even the most experienced candidates to completely overlook this golden opportunity to improve their ranking among all other applicable candidates. Most candidates completely blow right past this low-hanging fruit and miss an amazing opportunity to shine. This is why, when you use my technique for answering this question, you are going to stand out against all other candidates. The solution is simple and very practical.

Recently, during a consulting workshop that I was providing for a Fortune 50 company, I utilized this example to demonstrate the importance of being a communicator that is receiver-focused. I asked the twenty participants in the room how many of them have ever interviewed another person before to hire them for their organization. Eighteen of the twenty participants raised their hands. I asked them the typical responses they received when asking candidates why they wanted to work with the organization and their answers were nearly identical to the list I referenced in my example above ("I want to grow, I like the benefits, it will be good for my career, etc.").

However, I asked that same group of twenty top professionals what they desired most to contribute in their career. I asked them to raise their hands only if the following attributes were true for what they desire to do in any career that they are involved in. I listed four attributes including:

- Contributing their best skills & experiences every day to help the team reach its goals and objectives
- Developing team members and helping them to align around a common vision or goal
- Collaborating with others and having a leadership style that compliments the departments culture
- Moving their projects and initiatives forward while accomplishing results on time and under budget

The response from the participants was overwhelming. All twenty participants raised their hands and one person even said out loud, *"That is what I would like to accomplish every day in my work."* I said to these participants, *"If these are the things you would like to accomplish in your career, might it be wise to state these attributes when asked the question, 'Why do you want this position?'"*

We created a chart that represented both approaches to answering this question. On one side of the chart, they could see that all the answers that are typically offered for this question were self-centered. On the other side of the chart, they noticed that the answers were all "company" centered and receiver-focused. What shocked them the most is that both answers were true and authentic. They realized that they truly do want a job that they can contribute their best skills, accomplish the goal, and develop other people. In doing so, they realized that most people miss-interpret this interviewing question to be, "What are all the ways that I will personally benefit by getting this job?" Many participants were a gasp when they realized that this question is best interpreted, "What would you like to give to this company that will make you feel most fulfilled in this position?" Armed with this new perspective, these participants were equipped with a much more powerful anecdote to the question, "Why do you want this position?"

Advanced interviewers understand that to Nail the interview, the interviewee has to focus on *GIVING not GETTING*.

To absolutely *nail* the answer to this question, all you have to do is simply shift your focus away from how <u>YOU</u> will benefit from being hired and onto the benefits the <u>ORGANIZATION</u> will receive if they hire <u>you</u>.

Here is an example of what this answer might look like when the candidate uses this strategy:

> **Interviewer**: *"Why do you want this position?"*
> **Candidate**: *"I really believe that this is the perfect position to leverage all my best skills and talents to help the organization reach its goals. I feel that I can really contribute to the team given my background and experiences in this field and that my leadership style will compliment the leadership style and culture of the organization. One of my strengths is developing team members and getting them to align around a common goal. I believe I can get the team to rally around the key initiatives that we need to conquer in the coming months. I have a track record of hitting the ground running and learning fast while moving the business forward and I would like to do that for your department as well. I have a passion for this role and I would be privileged to serve the organization in this capacity."*

Please note that this is only one example for how you can answer this question with a receiver-focused response. As with all the examples in this book, this example is meant to be a framework into which you insert your specific skills and true experiences. Every candidate must personalize their answers with what is true and accurate for them and utilize verbiage that fits their own personal style and character. However, when candidates utilize this simple yet effective approach, the answer sounds so incredibly compelling that interviewers cannot even articulate why it sounds so much better than the typical responses they hear. They simply share that, for some reason, they felt the candidate that answered using this approach seemed much more professional and more experienced. I always smile when I hear this from the interviewers because the candidates that use this technique simply shifted their response from "what I will GET" to "what I can GIVE." They made their answer all about the <u>organization</u> and how they will benefit from hiring them for the position. What a concept! When a candidate makes it clear that they are interviewing to help the Hiring Manager succeed and to serve the organization vs. making the interview all about them, it always plays in their favor. Additionally, it is always humorous to me that the interviewers see candidates who utilize this approach as more "professional." Perception is reality in the interview process, and interviewers perceive candidates who leverage this approach (receiver-focused) as more professional than candidates who utilize the typical (self-focused) approach to answering this question. Given this information, it would be wise for you to leverage this knowledge and shift to a receiver-focused approach in the interview.

After studying the effects of this simple technique, I am amazed at how well it works and how it can really help a candidate to stand out from the crowd. It is time for you to obtain the position that you have worked so hard to achieve and this technique alone will have a huge positive impact toward that outcome.

During my live seminars, I perform an exercise in the room to further reinforce the power of this concept. I want candidates to get the basic concept that when this question is answered with the typical response, how it appears to be so self-centered. I have two people come to the front of the room and sit facing each other. One acts as the interviewer while the other acts as a candidate interviewing for a job. I then hand the interviewer 5-6 markers and I have them hand the candidate a marker every time the candidate says something that sounds self-centered. I then have the candidate answer with the first sample verbiage I provided above: "**I** want...," "...great company **for me**...," "....**help me** to build....", "...**help me** to gain...," "...**I** can learn...," and "...**I** can benefit..." One by one, the interviewer hands the candidate marker after marker. This exercise helps to demonstrate to the audience how the interviewer must give something to the candidate in order for them to receive all the benefits they hope to gain from getting the job. By the end of the exercise, the candidate is holding all the markers (after all, it really is all about <u>them</u>, right?). Then, I do the exercise in reverse. I hand the markers to the candidate and I ask the interviewer to take a marker from the candidate every time the candidate make a statement that sounds like the organization will benefit from hiring the candidate as they answer this question. The candidate starts answering the question utilizing the technique (Give not Get) and verbiage that I recommended in the second example above, including statements like "...my skills will <u>help the organization</u>...," "...I can <u>contribute to the team</u>...," and "...I will <u>serve the organization</u>...," and "...help develop the team..." Statement after statement, the interviewer reaches out to receive a marker and by the end of the exercise, the interviewer is holding all the markers. The simple shift from seeking "to serve, rather than be served" revolutionizes the interview. These candidate are positioned so far above other candidates that interviewers cannot help but feel that even the "atmosphere" in the interview was more collaborative when the "Give not Get" approach is utilized. It has been my experience that candidates who tap into this technique find that they are "winning" the interview game and are being offered positions they never seemed to be offered in the past.

There is one additional thing you should consider. This technique is so powerful because it shifts the candidate's perspective from "self serving" to "serving others." My consulting firm is now discovering that when candidates also adopt this strategy not only during the interview process, but also in their daily role when they do get the job they are interviewing for, they assimilate faster to the culture of the organization and report that they are finding themselves more fulfilled in their career. As a result, I find this approach to not only be a powerful and effective interviewing strategy, but perhaps a "natural law" that serves the betterment of all involved. You may find that this "servant leadership" approach not only resonates well with the leaders of your organization, but also find that you are sleeping better at night and waking up with greater energy in the morning to accomplish your work.

Last, remember that when wanting to grow within an organization, you are always interviewing. This is the perfect way to set yourself up well for promotional opportunities. Every meeting you attend, every project you work on, and every accomplishment you achieve becomes the experiences you will reference in your next interview for a promotion. In fact, interviewers often want to know what your plan of action will be when you get the job. Having a well thought out answer to this important question will be critical for the success of your next interview. As a result, in the next chapter I'll share some additional tips and techniques for how best to share your plan of action that will cause you to stand out from the crowd and absolutely nail the interview.

Now It Is Your Turn:

Below, clearly articulate what skills, attributes and experiences that you bring to the table to help the organization reach its goals (how you can *Give*). Write out your response and practice this verbiage prior to your next interview. Please note that the skills, attributes and experiences that you list may change from interview to interview depending on the position that you are applying for in the moment. As a result, you will want to update these elements in preparation for each new interview.

Interview Question: *"Why Do You Want This Position?"*
Ways that I can articulate how I can Give (vs. Get)

KEY #3: ALIGNMENT

In this chapter, we will discuss how to prepare for and respond to another one of the most commonly asked questions in the interview, *"What is your plan of action ('ninety day plan') should you be selected for this position?"*

There are two common pitfalls that candidates fall into when attempting to answer this question in their interviews. The first pitfall is "lack of clarity." The second pitfall is "absolute clarity with a plan that is too prescriptive." Let's explore each of these further.

Pitfall #1: Lack of Clarity

The first pitfall that candidates fall into when answering this question (and almost any question, for that matter) is lack of clarity. Candidates frequently share with me that they had a general thought in mind as to how they would answer this question. They have a few ideas rattling around in their head and feel confident that they will be able to pick the right one when the time comes. However, when the question is finally asked and it is time for the candidate to speak, they feel stuck and often get tongue-tied. As a result, they pause and then begin to stammer, stutter, and struggle to spit out a practical answer. When the candidate is unclear on their answer, they use verbal fillers, "uhs" and "ums," to stall. It is also at this time that the candidate frequently uses *soft* language when describing their plan. They often use words like "kinda," "probably," "maybe," and "sorta."

> **Interviewer**: *"What is your plan of action (ninety day plan) if you get this position?"*
>
> **Candidate**: *"Hmmm, good question. For me, I, uh...think that, ummm, a plan is important. Uhhh, I would probably, you know, kinda bring the team together. I want to kind of know more about them. Oh, and I maybe want to take them on a tour of each location and sort of help them learn each, uhhhh, process and location, you know. I also want to make sure they are somewhat familiar with, you know, our goals and have at least maybe a little clarity around our objectives. I probably also want to spend a little time learning what some of your, like, priorities are and ensure that team members are kind of in alignment with some of those priorities."*

I coined a phrase to describe the mental struggle that individuals have when trying to process their thoughts in the interview. I call it "Racquetball Mentality." For example, candidates often share with me that they have several ideas for how they may answer a particular question bouncing around in their head. These ideas, like multiple racquetballs on a racquetball 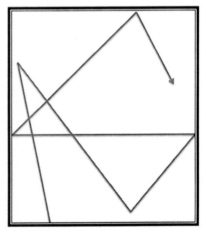 court, our bouncing off the walls of their brain and flying around their mental court at lightning speed (see graphic).

When two key ideas for answering a question are bouncing around in their brain, it gets a bit busy. When three ideas are bouncing perpetually off the walls of their brain, it gets a bit crowded. When four or more ideas are ricocheting off the walls of their brain, it gets very confusing.

"Racquetball Mentality"

Lacking a clear strategy for how to answer an interview question, candidates often get confused in the moment as to which of these "racquetballs" to choose from. They pause, use verbal fillers, and soft language as they diligently try, in the moment, to select which racquetball to grasp and utilize as their answer to the interview question. By the time they make their mental selection, they have already inadvertently communicated to the interviewer that they are unsure, unclear, and unable to succinctly articulate their thoughts. Their plan of action for the first ninety days, at this point, becomes second in importance to the insight the interviewer has gained about this candidate and how the candidate most likely communicates in high stress situations. The position the interviewer is filling is almost *always* what is considered a high stress position (of course, do you know many that aren't?).

What is even worse is the fact that even if their answer from that point forward incorporates a solid ninety-day plan, their initial hesitation and inability to quickly and clearly articulate their plan causes the interviewer to wonder if they will also struggle daily on the job if they hire this individual for the position. Therefore, it is absolutely imperative to be clear on how you will answer your questions in an interview. One phrase that I have coined to help candidates remember the importance of this process in the interview is "Clarity Cures Confusion." When you have clarity, all the "noise" we hear in our brains fades into the background and the conviction with which a candidate speaks is so much more powerful and passionate. To help a candidate gain clarity, they must determine what they want to say and how they want to convey it. This process is not about memorization (in fact, I discourage memorizing an interview answer as it looks robotic and mechanical in an interview). Instead, it is about being resolved as to the point you are wanting to make and saying it with confidence and clarity.

"Clarity Cures Confusion"
You must get clear on which point (racquetball)
you will reference during the interview and
bring that point to the forefront.

As you prepare for your interview, it is absolutely critical for candidates to get clear on their strategy for answering each of the interview questions that arise. Selecting the "racquetball" answer prior to the interview (and blocking out all other options by bringing that point to the forefront) not only supplies you with clarity, but also gives you confidence and peace of mind that you know ahead of time what you will say. When you know what you will say in advance of the interview, it changes how you say it, to include greater confidence, better direct eye contact, and stronger word choice.

In all of the years that I have been video-recording candidates as they prepare for their interview, one thing vividly stands out. When candidates know, in advance, what they are going to say, they tend to use what I call "Power Language." They tend to use more superlatives and their statements are more definitive. For example, a candidate who is clear tends to say things like, *"I am confident that I can accomplish this task"* and *"This is exactly how I will tackle this challenge."* When they are struggling with the "Racquetball Mentality," they tend to say things like, *"I am fairly confident that I can pretty well accomplish this task"* and *"This is how I think I might go about it."*

When a candidate is clear, the interviewer is clear. When the interviewer is clear, it plays heavily in the favor of the candidate. In fact, it is helpful for candidates to know that if you desire for your interviewers to be clear that you are the best candidate for the position, you have to first be clear as to why you are the best candidate for the position. You must also have effective strategies for articulating your responses clearly and concisely. While this is true for every interview question, it is especially imperative when answering the question, *"What is your plan of action (ninety day plan) should you be selected for this position?"*

Pitfall #2: Absolute Clarity With A Plan That is Too Prescriptive.

Another pitfall that candidates fall into when answering this question is that of "absolute clarity with a plan that is too prescriptive." Candidates frequently focus on the specific detailed actions they will take and changes they will make within the department when they get hired. Candidates often <u>tell</u> the interviewer what the first five or so projects and/or key actions and changes they will employ within the first ninety days. In doing so, they believe they are impressing the interviewers with their ability to create a plan, make things happen and drive for results. Using this line of thinking, below is an example of what a candidate might say in response to this question:

> <u>Interviewer</u>: *"What is your plan of action (ninety-day plan) if you get this position?"*
> <u>Candidate</u>: *"Well, I have done my homework and I know exactly what I will do. First, I will hire someone to help us with administrative tasks and duties so that my team and I can focus on the really important things that actually matter to the organization. Also, the reports right now are too long and too busy to add value. I will streamline the reports and take out anything that does not add value so that we can stay focused. Last, I will sit down with each of my direct reports and let them know that our work is going to look a lot different from now on. I will share with them that I will be holding them accountable for high performance, which is something they are not currently used to because their previous manager was not as effective as they could be. That is exactly what I will do during the first ninety days on the job."*

Let's review the above answer. I want to be clear as to why I believe this answer perfectly exemplifies the pitfall into which candidates so easily fall when referencing their ninety-day plan.

Having a strong and powerful plan for <u>*what*</u> the candidate will do for the first ninety days is important, if not critical. But <u>*how*</u> they answer the question plays a critical role as to how the interviewer receives the plan. Some candidates experience the opposite of the "Racquetball Mentality." Some candidates experience what I call "Anchor Mentality." They have selected the "racquetball" idea that they are going to speak on during the interview. Well done. After all, clarity cures confusion, right? However, these candidates make two fatal errors.

Be Cautious of "Anchor Mentality"

First, after determining what ninety-day plan they will reference in the interview, they describe their plan with such great detail that it appears to leave little room for input and sugges-tions from others. They become *so* prescriptive as to exactly what their ninety-day plan will entail  that it appears that few people would be able to advise them otherwise. Candidates often tell us that they were prescriptive with their answers because they wanted to show the interviewer that they were intelligent, forward-thinking, strategic, and clear. Instead, interviewers often see can-didates that are too prescriptive in their answers as stubborn, arrogant, unwise and uncoachable.

Second, after selecting exactly what their ninety-day plan will entail and describing it in great detail, they speak of their plan with such convic-tion that one would assume they believe it is the only great plan that exists. When the candidate uses such words as "I know _exactly_ what I will do" and "I _will_ streamline the reports," interviewers often assume that they are so determined to enact their plan that they, as the Hiring Manager, may have no say as to how that plan is enacted and what additions or changes they might advise be incorporated throughout the process. Additionally, the plan that is described may not be what the Hiring Manager would like to see happen in their department. Candidates often tell me that they spoke their ideas with such conviction because they wanted the interviewer to know they are a person of integrity who will make things happen and follow through with their ideas.

The problem with these two fatal errors is that it leaves most interviewers with the belief that this candidate has essentially tied an anchor to their idea and will remain immoveable to other potentially better possibilities. Yes, they may believe that the candidate is intelligent, forward-thinking, strategic, and clear. They may also believe that the candidate is a person of integrity who will make things happen and follow through with their ideas. However, the candidates highly prescriptive ideas spoken with such great conviction often leaves interviewers believing that this individual is perhaps not coachable, possibly "maverick" in their style, and may be so insistent that their way is the only way, which could make tenured team members in their existing department frustrated and disengaged. In effect, this candidate's approach may ultimately be an "anchor" that slows progress and drags everyone down in the Hiring Manager's department.

The key here is that it could leave doubt in the interviewer's mind that this candidate can work effectively with others. This single doubt is often what causes candidates to hear, *"You interviewed well; in fact, you were our number two candidate. However, we just felt another individual was a little more applicable for this position."* Is it a logical and fair assessment on the part of the interviewer to assume the other candidate was more applicable than you? Maybe or maybe not. But it does not seem to matter as it is a reality of the assumptions made by interviewers every day. Interviewers make these assumptions all the time because they often have not had a chance to actually see you perform on the job. As a result, the interview is the only experience they have with the candidate. Therefore, their best prediction of what you will be like to work with if you get the job is how you are communicating with them right now in the interview.

An interviewer's best prediction of how you will perform on the job tomorrow is how you are performing in the interview today.

That is worth repeating. Remember, an interviewer's best prediction of how you will perform on the job tomorrow is how you are performing in the interview today.

In one of my "Advanced Interviewing Strategies" workshops, one of the participants who heard this concept yelled out in the middle of the seminar, "Congratulations, number two!" She had been told this many times herself in previous interviews and recognized the "Anchor Mentality" that had pulled her down in the interview process. It was an epiphany for her. This fatal error has destroyed opportunities for many candidates along their interviewing path. Don't let "Anchor Mentality" weigh you down in your interviews. Instead, use a strategy that I have found to be far more effective in the interview process and resonates best with most interviewers.

The strongest response (out of hundreds of possible answers I have heard to this question) centers around the concept of *alignment*.

This third key to crushing the interview is so profound that many interviewers have told me that they have noticed that the candidate who answers this question utilizing the *alignment* strategy to be the candidate that is seen as the "best fit" for the position. However, when they hear the above typical responses to this question (due to either the "Racquetball

Mentality" or the "Anchor Mentality"), they often feel this candidate is not quite ready to take on the responsibilities of the role. Why is that?

Some candidates find it difficult to focus on any one potential solution and seem to have a great deal of difficulty defining it in clear terms ("Racquetball Mentality"). They express their *general thoughts* surrounding their potential plan in such a non-assertive way that many interviewers make the assumption that this person is not self-directed (and "self-directed" is a common key characteristic desired for most positions). Dealing with someone who is not assertive, not self-driven, and are unclear on what the necessary steps will be in their new role can be challenging (at best) and almost always leads to more work for the hiring manager.

Some candidates, on the other hand, focus all their energies on exactly what they will <u>achieve</u> during their first ninety days on the job and share it in very prescriptive terms ("Anchor Mentality"). They want to impress their interviewer with their understanding of the role and to prove that they are ready to "hit the ground running." They share elaborate plans for taking the business to a whole new level. The interviewer, however, finds this form of response to be too rigid and immovable, causing them to believe this candidate may be too difficult to reign in once they are in the position. Dealing with someone who is not teachable or coachable may actually lead to more work for the Hiring Manager.

The alignment approach to this question, however, reinforces to the interviewer that what is most important to the candidate is understanding what is most important to the Hiring Manager and all key stakeholders involved with the department. The candidate centers their focus on <u>aligning</u> with the Hiring Manager to ensure they know and understand all goals and objectives for the position and the department. They express their desire to <u>align</u> with the key stakeholders and understand their pain-points and how best to serve the needs of key clients and customers.

They point out the importance of <u>aligning</u> with their direct reports to understand their skill levels and become aware of their developmental requirements. They reference the need to <u>align</u> all team members around a common purpose to ensure they are all focused on the right goals and objectives.

<u>Alignment</u> is the key to your ninety-day plan.

Here is an example of a more effective response to this question in the interview:

<u>Interviewer</u>: *"What is your plan of action (ninety-day plan) if you get this position?"*

<u>Candidate</u>: *"Having a ninety-day plan is crucial for success in any role. For me, the first thing I would do is sit down with the Hiring Manager and make sure I understand how they our department fitting into the overall vision and mission of the organization. For my particular role, I want to align with my manager to ensure I gain their perspective on my key initiatives and establish clear priorities. I also want to sit down with my direct reports and assess each of their areas of strengths as well as their areas for development. It will also be important that we are all focused on common goals and objectives. Last, I would sit down with my peers and stakeholders. It will be important for me to build strong relationships with each of them and ensure we are all aligned and heading in the same direction. Given all of these things, I would ensure that I am aligned with my direct manager and together develop the vision and strategy that will help us to meet all our objectives and ensure our success."*

The *alignment* strategy offers the candidate a clear and concise way to confidently articulate their plan while also being completely open to the advice, input, and recommendations of their direct manager as well as all other key stakeholders. The candidate is both confident <u>and</u> humble. They have a clear plan that first serves the Hiring Manager, direct reports, peers, and stakeholders. This approach helps the candidate to neither appear wavering nor set in their ways. Instead, this approach helps a candidate to frame their answer in a way that demonstrates their ability to think strategically while also being interpersonally savvy enough to understand the importance of aligning with the very individual who is working to hire the right person into this key role (the Hiring Manager).

Interviewers who experience the alignment answer from candidates often state they feel that the candidate is "service-minded, focused on the right things, and committed to ensure the department succeeds." As a result, the interviewers simply often use the phrase for these candidates, *"I just feel like they are the best 'fit' for the job."* This third key to crushing the interview (alignment) is just one more way to ensure that when it comes to questions regarding your ninety-day plan, you have absolutely *"nailed it!"*

<u>Now It Is Your Turn:</u>

Below, clearly articulate your plan of action (ninety-day plan). Write out your response to describe what you will do during the first three months on the new job and how you will gain ***Alignment*** with your boss, peers, direct reports, and others. Then practice this verbiage prior to your next interview. Please note that the plan of action (ninety-day plan) that you choose to share in your next interview may change from interview to interview depending on the position that you are applying for in the moment. As a result, you will want to update these plans in preparation for each new interview.

My Ninety-Day Plan *(Alignment* **is the key***)*

_____

_____

_____

_____

_____

_____

_____

_____

_____

_____

_____

_____

_____

_____

_____

_____

_____

KEY #4: SHORT – LONG – SHORT

Most interviewers ask the question, "What are your short-term and long-term goals?" This question can often separate one candidate from another and help them to win the interview. However, most applicants do not have an effective strategy to navigate the answer to this important yet challenging question.

As with most interview questions, candidates often spend their entire "prep" time thinking about their potential answer to these questions in their head and never really landing on a pre-determined strategy for nailing their response. Instead, they ponder awhile and consider a few words they may use when answering this question, but never really develop a written plan for what they will say when it arises. As a result, the interviewer asks the candidate, *"What are your short-term and long-term goals?,"* and the candidate's brain immediately locks up. Then, in that moment, they hear the whispers of two primary voices in their head. These two voices play a critical role throughout the entire interview process.

After interviewing and video-recording countless interviewees (that range from college graduates to NFL Prospects and Vice Presidents of multi-billion dollar corporations), I have captured and witnessed on video the non-verbal expressions that candidates make when they hear these two voices in their heads during the interview. I have labeled these two voices the "file clerk" and the "construction worker with a bullhorn."

Candidates hear two primary voices in their head during the interview process: The "File Clerk" and the "Construction Worker With a Bullhorn"

The voice of the "file clerk" in our head is the one that is searching through the countless files of our brain to pull out effective answers, applicable responses, and practical examples that we can use when responding to interview questions. These files are very comprehensive, often disorganized, and challenging to locate. The "file clerk" in our head is often scatter-brained and frantic during the interview. They are on "stand-by" and as each question is asked, they fly into motion and start scrambling to find the right file to give to you so that you can articulate your answer clearly and succinctly.

However, finding the right file can take some time. As a result, the "file clerk" often whispers to the candidate, *"That file is here somewhere but I cannot seem to find it right now. Stall for a moment. Try some small talk until I can locate it."* On video, the non-verbal cues that this process is taking place are very evident. I will often see the candidate look up to the ceiling, begin to fidget, and stammer as they nervously await the "file clerk's" response. The answer to this question frequently sounds like this.

Interviewer: *"What are your short-term and long-term goals?"*
Candidate: (looking at the interviewer) *"Yes. I, uh, do feel that having,*
umm, short and long-term goals is important. (looking down at resume)
Goals help us to, you know, be prepared and we need them to, uh, you
know, to be successful. So, for me, (now looking to the left and up at
the ceiling) *my short and long-term goals consist of...and these are in no*
particular order ... uhhhhh ....."

While answering the question, this candidate's eyes are shifting from
the ceiling, to the table, and to the side of the room. Suddenly, after several moments of stammering, they look the interviewer straight in the
eye and speak with much greater conviction. Why? Because the second
primary voice in their head spoke louder and with more authority than
the "file clerk."

The "construction worker with a bullhorn" is the second primary voice
candidates hear in their head. The "construction worker with a bullhorn"
is wearing a hard hat, is serious about his work, and is on a strict deadline.
The "construction worker" is impatient, is holding a stopwatch in one
hand and a bullhorn in the other, and is responsible for pace and productivity. He realizes that every second counts and is prepared to keep things
moving forward at all cost. He has a bullhorn and he is _not_ afraid to use it.

It is very evident on video when a candidate in the interview hears
the voice of the "construction worker with a bull horn" in their head. This
individual will be stammering and fumbling for an answer and, after several "uhs" and "umms," will suddenly look the interviewer square in the
eye and speak their answer with clarity and conviction. The "construction
worker with a bullhorn" saw that the "file clerk" was not being productive
nor getting the job done, so he used the bullhorn and shouted in the ear

of the candidate, *"Say something, stupid, or your going to look like an idiot. Speak, you fool, <u>speak!</u>"*

In that moment, the candidate simply takes whatever incomplete files that the "file clerk" has offered and starts dictating them to the interviewer. These files are often incomplete, unclear, and out of order. The "file clerk" may periodically provide them with a little more detail while they are speaking, but by then, it is often too late. It becomes clear to the interviewer that the thought process behind the answer provided is weak, incomplete, and often sounds impromptu and "made up."

In the midst of the "hem-hawing" and "umming" that the first whisper encouraged, the candidate hears the second whisper in their head and finally feels the urge to speak whatever comes to the tip of their tongue because, after all, they will look stupid if they do not spit something out immediately, right? At least that is what the "construction worker with a bullhorn" convinced them to believe when he insisted they start speaking regardless of whether their thought process was clear or unclear. So they do. And when they do simply spit something out, it takes on a familiar tone that most interviewers have heard time and again. They start their response with a stall and use body language that clearly indicates they are not as prepared as they should be to answer this question. The message this sends to a professional interviewer is very clear, which is, *"If they are unprepared to answer this question now, what else will they be unprepared to answer if I hire them for this job?"* Then, the candidate suddenly obeys the second whisper they hear, which tells them to *"Speak!"* and the candidate abruptly shifts their tone and body posture and answers the question decisively. To continue from the first example, this is how it might sound in the interview.

Interviewer: *"What are your short-term and long-term goals?"*
Candidate: (looking at interviewer) *"Yes. I, uh, do feel that having, umm, short and long-term goals is important.* (looking down at resume) *Goals help us to, you know, be prepared and we need them to, uhhhhh, you know, to be successful. So, for me,* (now looking to the left and up at the ceiling) *my short and long-term goals consist of... and these are in no particular order ... ummm, ..."* (Pause...then a sudden change of posture and eyes shift from the ceiling to the interviewer) *"my short-term goal is to get a good job with a stable company and learn as much as I can and my long-term goal is to be a Vice President within the next three years."*

The message this sends to the professional interviewer is quite clear. Hiring managers & recruiters often state, *"If they were unprepared and then suddenly shift to a declarative posture now, what other decision will they be so 'maverick' with when they get this position?! When they don't know the answer to something in their new role if I hire them, will they simply make it up 'off the cuff' and insist that it is the best solution?!"*

When this occurs, interviewers often make the assumption that this candidate may not be the best "fit" for the position. Why? Because the person that fills <u>this</u> position must be a strong communicator with a clear vision and the ability to articulate their thoughts well to the people they work with and for. This is an assumption that is fatal to great candidates who are both ready and able to do the job. However, without a clear strategy for answering this question, a great candidate is vulnerable to the *voices* in their head that prevent them from standing out from their competition and being viewed as the top candidate for the role.

Candidates who watch their own interview on video are shocked that their mental processing is so visible to others. What is also surprising to them is that during the interview, they actually felt they answered the question "pretty well." Candidates will often view their own video and are flabbergasted to see their eyes shifting up to the ceiling or down at their paper and using all the typical verbal fillers like "um," and "uh," and "well, you see." In that moment, they understand the value of having a well thought out and prepared strategy for answering each of the top interview questions. What is even more amazing to me is the fact that this all takes place in the span of about 90 seconds!!

Candidates tend to make two fatal errors when it comes to the actual language they use to answer both the short-term and long-term goals question. I will address each of these questions separately and then we will combine them together at the end of the chapter. First, we will discuss both the typical answers and the most effective response a candidate can provide to the short-term goals question.

Fatal Error Part 1: Short-Term Goals That Are Too Passive or Too Aggressive

First, I will start with the typical answer to the short-term goals portion of this question. What is often heard in the short-term goals question is an answer that is soft and non-assertive. Candidates frequently state that their short-term goal is to *learn*. We all know that every single person that steps into a new role is going to learn. However, when a candidate states that their primary short-term goal is to *learn*, it sounds incredibly passive and non-committal.

Candidate: *"With regards to my short-term goals, I want to step into this role and learn as much as possible. I want to spend several months learning all that I can about the company, my boss, and the position that*

I am in. I really feel like the first several months will be a training ground for me and it will be important for me to soak in as much information as possible."

On the other hand, some candidates, out of their passion for wanting to appear both intelligent and driven, tend to be too aggressive in articulating their short-term goals. They may say things like this:

Candidate*: "With regards to my short-term goals, I know EXACTLY what I will do. First, I will update policies and completely change the accountability measures to ensure we are running a tight ship. Then I will immediately enforce a new policy surrounding the budgeting process to get us fiscally on track." Then I will ... and then I will .... and then I will...."*

Similar to the question regarding the ninety-day plan, candidates (out of their desire to appear knowledgeable and able to make change happen quickly) make the fatal error of being too aggressive, too specific, and too prescriptive about what they will accomplish in their new role. Some candidates will say to me, *"But I would try to do all those things and isn't it a good idea to show that I have done my homework and that I am willing to "hit the ground running?'"* While those attributes are healthy and strong, they are approaching their answer ineffectively. Let's analyze both the above answers and understand why these errors are so costly in the interview process.

There are several fundamental challenges with this candidate's initial answer to the interview question, *"What are your short-term goals?"* The First and foremost error in this approach is the fact that they did not have a written plan for how they would answer this question in the first place. While I never encourage a candidate to write down an answer to an interviewing question and bring it to the live interview, I always encourage candidates to write out their planned responses to key questions in advance of the interview during their prep time so they can effectively determine the general path down which they want to take the interviewers when answering a question. With a pre-planned response, the voice in their head that they hear from the "file clerk" now responds with, *"We planned for this question and I have the answer right here at my fingertips. In fact, I have already pulled the file, color-coded it, and placed it on the top of the file cabinet. Here you go!".*

Additionally, there is a fundamental "truth" that many candidates forget about when answering the short-term goals question, which is the fact that often the interviewers know more about the position and the past challenges that have been faced by individuals in this position than the candidate who is interviewing for the role (whether it be an internal or external candidate). The interviewers are also often familiar with most of the team members that work with or report to the position the candidate is applying for. As a result, when a candidate gives an aggressive and overly prescriptive plan for what they will do when they first receive the position, there is a risk that the candidate does not know all the parameters that influence the decisions of the past and the present (i.e. the VP does not support that approach, the team is resistant to the key measures that the candidate insists on using when they first get the job, the report that the candidate insists on changing was developed by the very person interviewing the candidate, etc.). Therefore this very detailed plan is considered "risky" by the interviewer without the candidate even realizing it. Some candidates ask, *"But if they think my plan is flawed or risky, they will tell me during the interview, right?"* The answer is emphatically NO! They will not tell you that your answer is flawed. In fact, our research shows they will do the opposite. They will smile, nod, perhaps even say the word "interesting." However, with very few exceptions, even in a major blunder interviewing moment, interviewers will not call you out on a mistake or botched answer. Rather, they will smile, nod, and give great eye contact (only to later say to the Hiring Manager, *"I do not recommend that we hire this individual."*).

They will not "call you out" or challenge you in the moment for a number of different reasons. Primarily because they a.) Do not want to embarrass you, b.) Do not want to appear like a "mean-spirited person," and c.) They realize that you have given them the gift of knowing who they <u>do not</u> want to hire. Instead, when the interview is over, they will shake your hand and say, *"I really enjoyed speaking with you today."* Then you will go home feeling good about the interview, sit by the phone, and wonder why you never hear from them again. Or worse. They do call you and say, *"You did a great job. Unfortunately, we did feel we had another more applicable candidate that we hired. However, you were one of our top two candidates and I am confident you will find something else soon!"*

Why, you might ask, is that worse?! Because these candidates, having been told multiple times that they were "one of the top two candidates" will <u>*never*</u> feel the need to change their interviewing approach. Instead, they will continue to utilize the same interviewing techniques they used in their most recent interview and wonder why they are (what one of my workshop participants described herself as) "always a bridesmaid and never a bride." She stated that she always seemed to receive good feedback but consistently did not receive the position/promotion. As I mentioned in an earlier chapter, Einstein said it best when he coined the phrase, "Insanity equals doing the same thing over and over again and expecting different results." Yet interviewing candidates do it all the time. Because they are told they had a "good" interview, they do not change their approach. Author Jim Collins, in his book <u>*Good to Great*</u> reminds us all that "the enemy of

'Great' is 'Good.'" You do not want to be a *"good"* candidate. You want to be a *"great" candidate* (that is why you are reading this book right now). There is a *great* way to answer the short-term goals question that will help you to win over the interviewer and it is time that you know a more advanced strategy for *nailing* this question.

When asked the question, *"What are your short-term goals?,"* candidates often make the initial mistake of thinking that this question is designed to test their knowledge about the role and their willingness to drive results. They error in believing that the interviewer wants to know whether or not they know <u>what</u> to do if they get the job and whether or not they can quickly make the right changes. As a result, the candidate often shares short-term goals and plans that are extremely aggressive and lofty (without knowing the history of why things are the way they are today).

However, often what interviewers truly want to know when asking this question is "are you committed to this role and can you collaborate with others when it comes to the things you want to accomplish?" When answering with the five projects you plan to complete within two weeks of your first day on the job (which would typically take someone in this role six months or more to complete effectively), these answers cause interviewers to consider the possibility that you may be too "maverick" in your approach, may not fully understand what it takes to accomplish the task, and that you will run over a few people in the process (begging for forgiveness rather than asking for permission). The answer, however, that most interviewers are looking for is that you are excited and committed to this particular position and can work well with others to accomplish the task.

Most interviewers want to know less about the exact <u>tasks</u> you plan to accomplish and more about the <u>process</u> by which you will accomplish them.

What our research has unveiled is the fact that most interviewers want to know less about the exact tasks you plan to accomplish and more about the process by which you will accomplish your tasks. One of the best ways to answer the short-term goals question is to share your plan for *HOW* you will go about your job and less about *WHAT* you will do when you get your job. What often impresses interviewers is how you will interact with your boss, peers, and direct reports when you are hired into the organization.

When candidates state, *"I will change the XYZ policy immediately, fire those that are not performing up to par, promote Betty to the Operations Supervisor role, and eliminate four of the seven reports that are generated by the department,"* it can sound too overly aggressive and very dictatorial. However, when a candidate shares that their short-term goals are to, *"align with their boss, partner with their peers, and collaborate effectively with their direct reports,"* the interviewer sees you as a leader that understands the importance of teamwork and building relationships with others rather than simply working on projects and checking the box. The trap here is the fact that the first approach is not a horrible response. Rather, it is a very "typical" response. Therein lies the problem. It is *typical* and you are reading this book because you want to be more than *typical*. I assert that you are aiming for a *"Nailed it"* response, which requires a completely different perspective and technique (although a perspective and technique that <u>can</u> be learned).

A "Nailed It" response to the short-term goals question:

There is a better strategy for answering this question that interviewers find far more compelling. A *"Nailed It"* response to the short-term goals question sounds like the following:

<u>Interviewer</u>: *"What are your short-term goals?"*

<u>Candidate</u>: *"I have several short-term goals and I am really excited about what I can do to serve the organization in this capacity. The first thing I want to do in this role is to meet with my boss and ensure that I am aligned with the vision that they have set for the department/division. I want to make sure we are both on the same page and that I am supporting all efforts to generate success. Next, I really want to get to know my team members and better understand their strengths and talents as well as the challenges that they face on a daily basis. This will allow me to better collaborate with each individual and to understand how I can best support their performance to ensure we succeed as a team. Last, I really want to partner with all my peers and understand both their pain points and their passions so that we can work together to drive results for the organization. With those things in place, we can develop the plans and goals for successfully working together, clearly communicating our plan and initiatives to the leadership team, and collaborating to accomplish those goals."*

You will notice this reply focuses more on *<u>HOW</u>* the candidate will accomplish the work and less on *<u>WHAT</u>* the candidate will do if they are selected for the position. This answer also demonstrates to the interviewer that the short-term focus is entirely on making sure that the whole team succeeds. As is the case throughout this book, this is simply an example and just sample verbiage. You will want to personalize and customize your own answer to this question so that it reflects your personality and style. Use verbiage that you feel comfortable with and always make sure that you focus on HOW you will accomplish your tasks and less on WHAT tasks you plan on accomplishing.

In addition to the fatal errors that occur with candidates when they articulate their answers to the short-term goals question, they equally botch their answers to the long-term goals question as well.

Fatal Error Part 2: Long-Term Goals That Are Unclear Or Too Lofty

The most common errors made when answering the long-term goals question can be deadly. The first error consists of the candidate being *unsure* of what they envision long-term for their career. This lack of clarity often shows up in both their verbal and non-verbal responses. A candidate's lack of clarity shows up in their difficulty articulating their future goals, which makes it appear that the candidate is not forward-thinking or strategic. When this happens, candidates often articulate long-term goals that are not in alignment with the role for which they are interviewing. For example, I was interviewing a candidate for a highly technical leadership role within a top Fortune 50 Company. He declared, *"After getting this job, my long term goals are to be in the business side vs. the technical side of the organization because that is where my greatest passion lies within the industry."* Because his long-term goal was not in alignment with the role for which he was applying (his greatest passion is NOT in working in the technical part of the business), each interviewing panel member believed that he would quickly get bored in the role for which he was interviewing and made the decision to no longer pursue him as a viable candidate for the position. This very qualified internal candidate was *shocked* to discover that he would not be receiving a second interview.

The second major error that a candidate makes when answering the long-term goals question can crush their chances of winning the interview. Candidates frequently try to impress the interviewer with goals that are too lofty. They often express their desire to be in a senior executive-level position within a very short period of time. When interviewers hear this over-stated response, they often conclude that the candidate is not truly interested in this "lower" position for which they are interviewing, that the candidate is not experienced enough to know that it takes many years and hard work to move up that quickly in the organization, or that the candidate does not truly understand the organizational dynamics of their company and the process required for someone to realistically advance that far within it.

Without a clearly written plan in place prior to the interview, candidates have countless thoughts as to how they would answer this questions *swirling* around in their heads like paper debris in a tornado. These thoughts are rolling through their head and they feel as though they know what they are going to say until the moment comes and they, once again, here the dueling whispers in their head; one whisper telling them to "stall while they figure out how best to say what they want to say" and the other telling them to "hurry up and answer the question or they will look stupid!" As a result, they begin to speak but their answers are often very typically a.) Unclear and do not align with the position they are currently interviewing for in the moment, or b.) So lofty and too assertive that it causes the candidate to appear unrealistic with their perceptions of how quickly individuals advance within the organization. Both of these answers have a similar result and both of those results are negative.

While candidates are sometimes very savvy in their interpersonal communication skills, the most experienced recruiters and interviewers can quickly identify candidates that make these potentially fatal interviewing errors. A "***typical***" response to the long-term goals question often sounds like the following:

> **Interviewer**: *"What are your long-term goals?"* (for sake of this example, we will say this candidate is interviewing for a Store Manager position for a large company).
>
> **Candidate**: *"Ummm, long-term goals are important. I think it is, uhhh, critical to think about the future (looks at the ceiling as they await the "file clerk's" response) and what your own career aspirations are for yourself* (pause – now looks to the left as though searching for their answer somewhere in the room). *I'm, uh, you know, kind of a committed person who, like, makes things happen and I'll do, you know, whatever it takes to succeed.* (pause – now hears the "construction worker with a bullhorn" telling them to say something fast so they shift their eyes abruptly to the interviewer and speak louder and faster). *I like HR, Finances, and Marketing so long-term I see myself holding a VP role in one of these areas within three years."*

You may notice a couple of things occurred in this candidate's answer to the above question. First, they started with some filler language, which is the "stall" technique influenced by the "file clerk" in their brain (i.e. "Ummmm, long term goals are important...").

Then, as if on queue, the second whisper takes over and the candidate makes every attempt to impress the interviewer with how "smart and ambitious" they are. They share elaborate and lofty goals, which essentially has them being promoted from Manager to Vice President within three years of being hired by the organization. What candidates often fail to realize in their attempts to impress the interviewer is that the interviewer themselves may have been in a leadership role for over a decade and are still in a Director role aspiring to be a VP one day. All attempts to impress the interviewer backfire in that moment because the interviewer now perceives this candidate as both arrogant and impractical. Interviewers often make the connection that if the candidate is a bit arrogant and impractical when it comes to answering this question, how much more arrogant and impractical will they be when they are hired?

A "Nailed It" response to the long-term goals question:

The best answer to this question can be framed up in such a way that it is humble, realistic, and in alignment with the current role that the candidate is interviewing for in the moment. An example of a "***Nailed It***" response to the long-term goals question sounds like the following:

Interviewer: *"What are your long-term goals?"*
Candidate: *"With Regards to my long-term goals, once I have successfully met my goals in my current role and if I am fortunate enough to gain the endorsements and recommendations of my boss and other team members, I could see myself taking on more leadership responsibilities within the organization and growing with the company. I really enjoy this organization and would be honored to serve at higher levels within the corporation. All of those things, however, take a great deal of hard work, long hours, and many years to accomplish."*

Candidates who answer this question using this approach demonstrate several desirable characteristics that almost every interviewer is looking for in candidates that they interview regardless of the level and position.

First, a candidate who uses this approach to answering the long-term goals question demonstrates a passion and interest for the <u>current role</u> for which they are interviewing. In other words, they *REALLY* want to be at THIS company and working in *THIS* position! A candidate who utilizes this approach also demonstrates humility by expressing, *"...if I'm fortunate enough to gain the endorsements of my boss and other team members..."* Last, a candidate who utilizes this approach also expresses a realistic view of what is required to be promoted within the organization (i.e. "hard work" and "long hours"). When a candidate utilizes this strategy, the interviewer views the candidate as confident due to the fact that they have very high aspirations that are tempered by humility and a clear understanding of what it takes to succeed.

Now let's tie it all together.

While we just analyzed the short-term goals and long-term goals answers separately, they are most typically asked as a single question: "What are your short-term <u>and</u> long-term goals?" As a result, there is a strategy that assists candidates in nailing this two-part question and ensuring they position themselves as the best candidate for the job.

The key solution to an effective answer for the short-term and long-term goals question is a strategy I call "Short-Long-Short." Utilizing all the above recommendations within their answers, applicants also incorporate the "short-long-short" approach. Simply put, the candidate shares their short-term goals, then shares their long-term goals, and finally closes their answer by restating their short-term goals (thus the title, "Short-Long-Short").

The key solution to an effective answer for the short-term and long-term goals question is a strategy known as "Short-Long-Short."

When answering this question, the effective candidate starts off talking about their short-term goals with a focus on **HOW** they will accomplish their goals (align with boss, partner with peers, etc.) vs. **WHAT** they will accomplish in the role (change all processes, eliminate unnecessary reports, update training manuals, etc.). This assures the interviewer that the candidate is more focused on building relationships and establishing long-term business partnerships than they are on simply running everyone over to meet their own personal objectives.

When the candidate shifts to their long-term goals, I recommend that they remain high-level and speak in more general terms (i.e. "I would enjoy the opportunity to grow with the company" vs. "I want to be the VP in three years"). The purpose for staying high-level with this answer is to let the interviewer know that the candidate has aspirations for growing with the organization but that being promoted to the next level is not their primary focus. Why? Because when candidates spend a great deal of time talking about all their goals for moving up quickly within the organization and moving into executive roles in a very short period of time, the interviewer often becomes concerned that the candidate is not truly passionate about the role for which they are applying (it sounds to the interviewer as though this position would be more of a stepping stone for the applicant to get to the next level). Translated in "interviewer language," they ascertain that the candidate is more passionate about moving up in the organization than they are in fulfilling the duties of this role. While candidates often believe that letting the interviewer know that they plan to rise quickly to the next level of the organization will demonstrate their drive for success, it often causes the interviewer to feel that the candidate will not be happy in the current role that they are interviewing for and that they may get either frustrated or bored very quickly. As a result, the interviewer can easily misinterpret these statements to mean that the candidate does not truly want this role and that they will be interviewing new applicants within six months to a year to replace this person after they have moved to a different department or organization for bigger and better things.

Additionally, most candidates end this two-part question ("What are your short-term and long-term goals?) with their long-term goals. They believe this makes most sense and is in the most logical order. After all, they asked for my short-term and long-term goals and so I first gave them my short-term goals and ended with my long-term goals. However, I have discovered that there is a much more effective approach to closing out the answer to this question that effectively separates a candidate from all other prospects.

The effective candidate completes their answer to the short-term and long-term goals question by referencing back to their short-term goals and speaking about how excited (only when true and authentic) they are to work on specific projects that have been referenced thus far in the interview process and/or outlined in the job description. This reinforces the fact that while they desire to be with the company for a long time and could see themselves moving up in the organization if opportunities arise (therefore ambitious), they are most interested in stepping into the current position for which they are applying and accomplishing all the goals outlined for the role (therefore passionate about doing this particular job). This assures the interviewer that this candidate truly wants <u>this</u> particular role and has a passion for <u>this</u> specific position. Interviewers interpret this closing statement as a confirmation that the candidate is truly interested in this role and willing to stay in this position for a long time.

I call this approach the "Bungee Cord" effect. The candidate starts off talking about their short-term goals, then stretches forward to talk about their long-term goals, and finally springs right back to the short-term goals to remind the interviewer that they are one hundred percent focused on this position and passionate about fulfilling the duties of this role. The "Bungee Cord" effect has a profound impact on candidates who utilize this technique. Here's how the "Short-Long-Short" approach sounds in the interview process and why the "Bungee Cord" effect is so powerful in the interview process.

<u>Interviewer</u>: *"What are your short-term and long-term goals?"*
<u>Candidate</u>:
Short: *"I have several short-term goals and I am really excited about what I can do to serve the organization in this capacity. The first thing I want to do in this role is to meet with my boss and ensure that I am aligned with the vision that they have set for the department/division. I want to make sure we are both on the same page and that I am supporting all efforts to generate success. Next, I really want to get to know my team members and better understand their strengths and talents as well as the challenges that they face on a daily basis. This will allow me to better collaborate with each individual and to understand how I can best support their development within the organization. Last, I really want to partner with all my peers and understand both their pain points and their passions so that we can work together to drive results. With those things in place, we can develop the plans and goals for successfully working*

together, clearly communicating our plan and initiatives to the leadership team, and collaborating to accomplish those goals."

Long: *"Regarding my long-term goals, once I have successfully met my goals in my current role and if I am fortunate enough to gain the endorsements of my boss and other team members, I could see myself taking on more leadership responsibilities within the organization and growing with the company. I really enjoy this organization and would be honored to serve at higher levels within the corporation. All of those things, however, take a great deal of hard work, long hours, and many years to accomplish."*

Short: *"Until that time comes, though, my focus and my goals are to work hard in this position, grow my partnerships with my boss, direct reports, and peers, and to fully contribute in this current role to help the organization accomplish its goals. I personally cannot wait to get started on the XYZ project."*

Confidence and Humility Are The "Triumphant Twins"

The combination of confidence ("I have accomplished a lot in my career and I can absolutely achieve these goals") coupled with humility ("I will have to work hard, learn more, and I cannot do it without the help of all my direct reports whose talents and hard work are what make us so successful") creates a breakthrough in the walls of the interviewing fortress and establishes the gateway through which many candidates can successfully pass their most difficult interviews. In fact, I borrow a term from Tony Robbins when I call the demonstration of both confidence and humility in the interview the "Triumphant Twins." Additionally, when candidates are able to effectively *nail* both the short-term and the long-term goals question, it is easy to see how "The Stacking Effect" comes into play and how these advanced techniques begin to stack the deck in favor of the candidates who fully leverage each one of these advanced interviewing solutions.

Above and beyond these strategies, there are additional techniques that you can use to ensure that you stand out from the crowd as you interview for opportunities either within your current company or at another organization. In the next chapter, we will take a look at the next couple of interview questions (strengths and weaknesses) that often trip up candidates heading into the interview process. When you answer these questions with advanced strategies, it sets you apart as the best candidate for the position. After all, it is time that you master this game we call "the interview" and _nail_ every interview you participate in!

Now It Is Your Turn:

Below, clearly articulate your short-term and long-term goals. Additionally, clarify how you will utilize the "Short-Long-Short" strategy by closing with your short-term goals. Write out your response and practice this verbiage prior to your next interview. Please note that how you articulate your short-term and long-term goals may change from interview to interview depending on the position that you are applying for in the moment. As a result, you will want to update these goals in preparation for each new interview.

My *Short-Term Goals*

_____

_____

_____

_____

My *Long-Term Goals*

_____

_____

_____

_____

_____

_____

_____

How I Will Close With My *Short-Term Goals*

_____

_____

_____

_____

_____

_____

_____

KEY #5: MOST & LEAST

—◦◦◦—

There are few questions that trip up a candidate more than the question, "What are two or three of your key strengths and two or three of your weaknesses?" Strengths being articulated well in the interview are important for a successful outcome. Weaknesses, however, can quickly and decidedly make or break the interview.

The answers to these questions must be specific to the candidate and we always encourage every candidate to tell the truth. How a candidate frames up their answer, however, is critical. When you answer your questions in an interview, _what_ you say is not nearly as important as _how_ you say it. Sharing both your strengths and weaknesses clearly and confidently is absolutely critical to winning over the interviewer. We will review this question in two parts. First, I will review what I have found to be the best responses to the _Strengths_ question. Then, I will review what I have found to be the most powerful reply to the _Weaknesses_ question.

Part 1: Articulating Your Strengths

To understand how best to frame up your answer to the strengths question, it is important to understand what most candidates say when replying to this standard interview question. Over the last decade of helping candidates prepare for their interviews, I noticed that a clear pattern has emerged regarding how candidates answer questions regarding their strengths.

I frequently ask candidates what they will say when they answer the question, "What are two or three of your strengths?" The candidates smile, look me in the eye, and confidently tell me two to three key strengths that they bring to the table. Their smile is warm and their eyes are bright and they can quickly and confidently think of a few good strengths to share with me. We all like talking about our strengths and the candidate feels proud that they not only have some core strengths to offer the organization, they also feel proud that they could rattle them off quickly and confidently. Ah, a high point in the interview, right? Unfortunately, this is the very reason why so many great candidates fail to win the interview and receive the offer for the position. Let me explain.

When I work with a candidate, I often video record their initial interview (prior to any coaching or teaching) so that they can see how they appear to others. After the candidate has answered this question confidently, I will have them watch themselves on video and ask them how they performed on this question. Almost without exception, the candidates say, *"Wow, I did really well on that one, didn't I?!" It* appears to be a strong reply. After all, we can talk about our strengths all day long, right? However, the activity that I do with them next reveals to them why their response not only missed the mark, but also took what should have been a "bullseye" and turned it into a "botched" opportunity.

I place a piece of paper and a pen in front of the candidate. I then have them right the three strengths that they shared with me moments ago on the top of the paper.

My Strengths

- Good Communicator
- Care About People
- Organized

Next, I ask the candidate if they only have three strengths or if they have lots of strengths. They, of course, reply, *"I have a lot more than just three strengths."* As a result, I only give them about two minutes to write them all down and within a short time, they have ten or more strengths written down.

A Comprehensive List of My Strengths

- Good Communicator
- Care About People
- Organized
- Results Driven
- Team Player
- Influence Others
- Good Negotiator
- Develop Others
- Strong Presentation Skills
- Problem Solver

Once a list of all key strengths has been generated (the more the better), I have them pull out the job description of the position for which they are interviewing and ask them, *"If you were the interviewer, which three of these key strengths in numerical order would **most** benefit the person who acquires this position?"* The candidates often raise their eyebrows and begin to review their list of strengths from a different perspective. I have them place a "1" by the strength that would most benefit someone in this position, a "2" by the second most beneficial strength for this role, and a "3" by the third most beneficial strength that someone could bring to this position. Over eighty-five percent of the time, the candidate's list of the *most* beneficial strengths looks something like this:

My *Most* Beneficial Strengths

3* Good Communicator
- Care About People
- Organized

1* Results Driven
- Team Player
- Influence Others
- Good Negotiator

2* Develop Others
- Strong Presentation Skills
- Problem Solver

Candidates are often surprised to discover that the two or three (often all three) of the *most* beneficial strengths that they bring to this opportunity were not listed in the initial three strengths they originally rattled off when I first asked them to tell me their top three strengths. I also have found that candidates are more confident with their response to this question when they utilize this strategy because they are speaking about authentic strengths that they truly bring to the table (vs. trying to simply select a few that sound best for the position). Interviewers ask for a few key strengths, but what the candidate needs to hear in their head is, "What are three strengths that you bring to the table that are **MOST** necessary for the position you are applying for today?" This is why *"**Most**"* is part one of the 5th key to crushing the interview.

Typically, candidates are so anxious to share their strengths (finally something enjoyable to talk about in the interview) that they simply share a few strengths that first come to mind. The three strengths they shared were fine, but they were not the strengths that resonated *most* with the interviewer regarding the position they are trying to fill. When that occurs, an opportunity to truly shine in the interview is lost. It is common sense to focus on your strengths that most match the needs of the position for which you are applying, but it is <u>not</u> common practice.

Candidates must share their strengths that _MOST_ match the position for which they are applying. This is common sense but it is <u>not</u> common practice!

Always focus on your core strengths that match the needs outlined in the job description. In doing so, you set yourself apart as a top candidate for the position and the interviewer can begin to visualize you in this new position.

Part 2: Articulating Your Weaknesses

Weaknesses are another story all together. To understand how best to frame up your answer to the weakness question, it is important to understand what most candidates say when replying to this common question. Over the last two decades of helping candidates prepare for their interviews, I noticed that a clear pattern has emerged regarding how candidates answer questions regarding their weaknesses.

I frequently ask candidates what they will say when they answer the question, "What are two or three of your weaknesses?" The candidates immediately blush, shift their eyes down to the desktop, and say, *"I never know what to say when they ask this question."* I ask them if they have weaknesses and they chuckle and nod. We naturally hate talking about our weaknesses and the candidate feels shy about sharing anything that could make them appear to be negative or weak in the interview. Because we do not like to concentrate on anything negative prior to an interview (or any time for that matter), most candidates (if they are willing to be honest) spend little time getting clear on their weaknesses and specifically how they will speak about them in the interview. They simply trust that the "file clerk" will quickly and politely hand them the correct file during the interview and that, in the moment, they will just *"know"* what to say.

It is painful to watch at interview on video when the candidate is unfamiliar with an advanced strategy for answering the weakness question. The candidate may be doing fine in the interview up to this point and when the weakness question is asked, you see a complete shift in their physiology. Their eyes shift down, then to the side, then up to the ceiling as they shift in their chair and contemplate how best to articulate the things they do not do well. They rely on the "file clerk" who just put out a sign that reads "gone to lunch." They stammer, stutter, pause, and use a lot of filler words like, *"uh, um, you see, I think, kinda, sorta, sometimes, etc."*

Then, the "construction worker with a bull horn" wins out and they finally hear the voice in their head that states, *"Say something stupid or you are going to look like a fool."* And so they do. Without an advanced strategy to answer this question, the candidates take one of three primary approaches.

The first common approach candidates use to answer the weakness question is to use the age-old tactic of stating a strength but calling it a weakness. They may say something like, *"One of my key weaknesses is I care too much."* If you have not heard the news yet, let me inform you that the whole world knows this is an outdated gimmick that no longer works in the interview process. Interviewers and recruiters are onto your game and that trick of stating a strength but calling it a weakness no longer works. The nineties called and they want their interviewing strategy back!

The second common approach candidates utilize to answer the weakness question is to lie about their weaknesses. However, when candidates confess they simply made something up and then watch their recorded interview, they notice that almost every time their physiology gives them away. I had one candidate say to me, *"Look how I am fidgeting with my pen, looking at the ceiling, shifting in my chair – it is obvious that I am lying and if I were the interviewer, I would not hire me for that reason alone!"*

The third common approach candidates take when answering the weakness question comes from necessity more than choice. When they discover that the "file clerk" is unable to provide them with a good answer, the voice of the "construction worker with a bull horn" is screaming in their ear and telling them to speak. At that point, the only thing they have left to say … is the truth. So they tell the truth about some of their greatest weaknesses. They reveal their top two to three weaknesses, often at great length and in great detail. The actual response I received from a candidate to the weakness question sounded like this:

Interviewer: *"What are two or three of your weaknesses?"*
Candidate: (after staring at the ceiling for over 20 seconds, he slowly stated the following words) *"I...would...say... that...one of my...weaknesses...is the fact that I...have a tendency to struggle with some of the authoritative decisions that come down from the leadership of the organization and while it does not show in my work, it definitely shows in my demeanor in the workplace."*

As you can imagine, this candidate was unable to secure a position following his first several interviews. Why? Because the weaknesses he shared were devastating to his opportunity to acquire the position. After all, sharing weaknesses is one of the low points in the interview, right? Actually, when utilizing an advanced strategy for answering the weakness question, I have found that candidates can really separate themselves from the crowd and stand out as the top candidate when answering this question. There are three key strategies for nailing the weakness question.

The first key strategy to nailing the weakness question is clarity. When I work with a candidate, I often video record their initial interview (prior to any coaching or teaching) so that they can see how they appear to others. After the candidate has answered this question, I will have them watch themselves on video and ask them how they did on this question. Almost without exception, the candidate says, *"Oh man, that was horrible."* They hate that they have to talk about weaknesses and they loathe having to watch themselves talk about weaknesses on video. After all, who wants to talk about weaknesses, right? However, the activity that I do with them next reveals to candidates why having an advanced strategy for answering this question can make such a difference in their interview.

I, once again, place a piece of paper and a pen in front of the candidate (I bet this sounds familiar). I then have them right the two or three weaknesses that they just shared with me moments ago at the top of their paper.

My Weaknesses

- Impatient
- Frustrated easily
- Cannot delegate

Next, I ask the candidate if they only have three weaknesses. They, of course, chuckle and reply, *"No, I have about twenty million."* As a result, I only give them about two minutes to write them all down and within a short time, they have ten or more weaknesses written down.

A Comprehensive List of My Weaknesses

- Impatient
- Frustrated easily
- Cannot delegate
- Not Creative
- Do Not Like Confrontation
- Not Great With Numbers
- Perfectionist
- Overbearing
- Easily Distracted
- Antsy – Like to Be Moving

Once a list of all their weaknesses has been generated (the more the better as it provides a longer list to choose from), I have them pull out the job description of the position for which they are interviewing and ask them, *"If you were the interviewer, which three of these key weaknesses in numerical order would be **least** damaging to the person who acquires this position?"* The candidate, now understanding where we are heading with this activity, begins to review their list of weaknesses from a different perspective. I have them place a "1" by the weakness that would be least damaging to someone in this position, a "2" by the second least damaging weakness for this role, and a "3" by the third least damaging weakness that someone could bring to this position. Almost always, the candidate's list of the **least** damaging weaknesses looks something like this:

My *Least* Damaging Weaknesses

- Impatient
- Frustrated easily
- Cannot delegate

3* Not Creative

- Do Not Like Confrontation
- Not Great With Numbers

2* Perfectionist

- Overbearing
- Easily Distracted

1* Antsy – Like to Be Moving

Candidates are often surprised to discover that, once again, the two or three (often all three) of their *least* damaging weaknesses that they bring to this opportunity were not listed in the initial two to three weaknesses that they originally shared with me. I also have found that candidates are more confident with their response to this question because they are speaking about authentic weaknesses that they bring to the table. For the first time, many candidates realize that they can completely tell the truth with confidence knowing that their real weaknesses will not damage their chances to win the position. In fact, because the candidate can answer the weakness question with clarity and confidence, interviewers often respect them for being honest and open about the challenges they face. This is why *"Least"* is part two of the 5th key to crushing the interview.

The second key strategy for nailing the weakness question is how the candidate frames up their response. Most candidates jump right into their answer and begin sharing the most challenging facets of their personality. However, in my research on this topic, I have found that there is a way that the candidate can frame up their answer to this question by making a key observational statement up front. The observational statement that sets a more effective tone for their response is, *"I imagine we all have weaknesses and I certainly do as well. One of my weaknesses is...."* This single statement up front impacts how interviewers here the responses to the weakness question.

Working with countless interviewers over the last twenty years, I have asked interviewers what occurred to them when this statement was made in front of the weakness question. One by one, each interviewer told me that the first thing they immediately thought of was their own weaknesses. This statement made in front of a candidate's answer to the weakness question immediately creates a sense of relatability and connectedness for the interviewer. Most interviewers know that all candidates have weaknesses, and when this specific phrase is used, it creates instant connection that the interviewer feels with the candidate.

The third key strategy for nailing the weakness question is critical. It first requires an understanding that interviewers realize we all have weaknesses. The question is not whether or not you have weaknesses. We all have them. The real question is not even what your weaknesses are as a candidate. The interviewer is curious to know *what* your weaknesses are, but what they are even more interested in knowing is *how you overcome your weaknesses.* The power of this advanced interviewing skill is that you are sharing weaknesses that are authentic but emphasize more about how you are overcoming them as apposed to how these weaknesses are holding you back in your on-the-job performance.

This is one example of how the three keys strategies combined provide a powerful and effective response to the weakness question:

Interviewer: *"What are two or three of your weaknesses?"*
Candidate: *"Well, I imagine we all have weaknesses and I know I certainly do as well. One of my weaknesses is that I get antsy a lot. I do*

not like to sit still for long. I am one of those individuals who feel like they have to be on the go all the time. As a result, I always keep a daily planner with tasks to keep me focused and on track. Another weakness of mine is that I tend to be a bit of a perfectionist and I have realized that not everything needs to be absolutely perfect. To help me maintain a balance, I share the status of my projects with my Manager and I gain agreement with them on whether it is best to move on or to continue to hone the project and take it to a new level of excellence. I also have a peer that helps keep me accountable when I am spending too much time on something. Last, I would like to be more creative. I have friends that are incredibly creative and I wish I had more of that trait. In fact, whenever I am working on a project, I will reach out to many of my direct reports, peers, and other leaders to gain their perspective and to see if there is anything else we can do to make the project or initiative more creative."

Interviewers who hear this type of response to the weakness question often make an automatic assumption about this candidate. Interviewers frequently tell me, *"If this person is that open, honest, self-aware and confident about their weaknesses and have a plan for overcoming them, I can only assume they will do the same with the challenges they face on the job when we hire them."* Interviewers ask for a few weaknesses, but what they need to hear are weaknesses that are not damaging to your ability to do the job once you are hired. They are also less interested in what your weaknesses are and more interested in knowing whether or not you have a plan and strategy in place to overcome those weaknesses. Candidates have such anxiety when it comes to having to share their weaknesses (they sometimes state, *"I cannot tell them the real truth, can I?"*) that they simply fail to have a plan in place for how to share weaknesses clearly and succinctly.

Candidates must share weaknesses that are the _LEAST_ damaging to the position for which they are interviewing and share a plan for how they overcome those weaknesses.

Always focus on your strengths that are most beneficial to the role for which you are applying. Likewise, be sure to focus on your weaknesses that are <u>least</u> damaging to the position for which you are interviewing. In doing so, you set yourself apart as a top candidate for the position and the interviewer can begin to visualize you performing well in this position and working effectively with all the personnel in their organization.

There are several advanced strategies for nailing the interview and winning the job you most desire. As you can see, *"Most & Least"* is a crucial key to crushing the interview.

Now It Is Your Turn.

I have placed an area below for you to outline all your strengths and weaknesses and to determine which of these strengths and weaknesses you will share during your next interview. Please note that the strengths and weaknesses that you choose to share in your next interview may change from interview to interview depending on the position that you are applying for in the moment. As a result, you will want to update these rankings in preparation for each new interview.

My *Most* Beneficial Strengths

Rank   **Strength**

_____   _____

_____   _____

_____   _____

_____   _____

_____   _____

_____   _____

_____   _____

_____   _____

My *Least* Damaging Weaknesses

Rank   **Weakness**

_____   _____

_____   _____

_____   _____

_____   _____

_____   _____

_____   _____

_____   _____

_____   _____

KEY #6: RECENT & RELEVANT

—⟨∿∿⟩—

Another top 10 most frequently asked question in the interview is, *"Can you tell me about a time when you succeeded?"* Once again, candidates often let out a sigh of relief when they hear this question. They like to talk about the times that things went well. After all, it is much more fun to speak of the times we succeeded and the times at which everything seemed to fall in our favor.

Most candidates have several successes under their belt and could spend hours telling you all about the times that they succeeded. So, in the midst of the interview, the question is finally asked, *"Can you tell me about a time when you succeeded?"* The candidate smiles, feels confident in this moment, and begins to share a story from their past. And this is when, unbeknownst to the candidate, it often goes awry. Why? Because they tell the interviewer about a time when they succeeded but may not have used the advanced strategy that makes this moment shine for the candidate.

I was recently working with the Vice President of a multi-billion dollar grocery retailer. He was polished and poised. Nothing rattled this leader. He was preparing for his interview workshop that I was providing for their organization and I recorded his pre-workshop interview. Afterwards, I asked him how he felt about his interview and he said that he felt he did really well and that it is typically how he would interview for a new senior executive role. While he was reviewing his recorded interview that he gave in preparation for his next senior executive role in the company, this leader turned to me and started laughing uncontrollably. His answer to this question sounded something like this:

> **Interviewer:** *"Can you please tell me about a time when you succeeded?"*
> **Candidate:** *"I have succeeded many times in my career. I guess one that comes to mind is when I first became a Store Manager. I was working with a team that was struggling and the store performance was not what it should be. I rallied the troops, gathered my team, and created a new vision for us to move toward. I started developing each of my team members to ensure they knew what to do in order for our performance to improve. It was very successful and I was able to turn the situation completely around and we ended up being one of the most profitable stores in the system. When I look back on my career today, I am very proud of that achievement."*

At face value, most people would read the above statement and say, *"Wow, that sounds like a great answer – it is succinct, clear, and it outlines a great success that he had achieved."* However, this leader specifically called himself out at this part of the interview. Embarrassed, he looked at me and said, *"I did not really use that example, did I?!"* Why did he call himself out on this answer? Because he understood the power of the sixth key to crushing the interview.

He continued, *"I have over thirty years of experience with this organization and have accomplished many things along the way. Why would I take this moment and share a twenty year old success story?! It makes me look like I have not achieved anything else since that time!!"*

The wisdom of his words rings true. For the benefit of the additional participants in the room, I asked this leader to elaborate on his comment. He continued, *"I have successes in the past year alone that are ten times more powerful than this example. I am a Vice President who must be able to achieve important things to be ready to move to the next level. If the only success that I can think of is twenty years old, then other candidates who utilize* **recent** *examples must look much more appealing for this new role than I do."*

He explained further, *"The job description for my next role includes requirements like the ability to present and sell your ideas to board members, advanced negotiation skills, and the ability to solve complex challenges in a stressful environment. And here I am talking about developing store associates. Developing store associates is a good thing, but it is not* **relevant** *to the position that I am interviewing for next in my career. I did not nail this answer. In fact, I blew it!!"*

In that moment, this leader fully embraced the power of the sixth key to crushing the interview. When talking about a success story, two factors must be incorporated into your answer to make it profound and powerful. The two critical factors of an effective response to the success question is that the answer must include information that is both ***recent*** and ***relevant***.

**When talking about your greatest success,
the example must be both *RECENT and RELEVANT***

Many candidates, however, have so many thoughts swirling around in their heads that they get confused as to which story to share. They all seem good in the moment and unless you pre-determine which story is most recent and most relevant to the new role, the "file clerk" gets confused and hands you the first file that is pulled out from the cabinet. Unfortunately, the story is often interesting but has nothing to do with success in the new role and another golden opportunity to stand out from the crowd is lost to confusion. Why? The "Racquetball Mentality" that we discussed earlier eclipsed our reasoning and we went with the first story that popped in our minds. You must avoid the "Racquetball Mentality" and ensure you have a prepared answer to this question. This is an example of how this executive leader might answer this question today.

> **Interviewer:** *"Can you please tell me about a time when you succeeded?"*
> **Candidate:** *"I have been fortunate to experience many successes in my career. The one that comes to mind first is a project that we were working on eight months ago. In order for us to complete the purchase of another large grocery chain, I had to present several times to the board. I was able to influence them toward making this important and critical decision to move forward with the purchase. While there were very complex negotiations that had to take place with several parties involved with this acquisition, I was involved with each one of them and they were all completed on time and resulted in the negotiation term falling in our favor. There were many moving parts and I have an amazing team that rallied around this project to see it through. Some are calling it one of the most successful acquisitions of our company history and I'm so grateful to have played a central role in the success of this project."*

When a candidate is able to articulate a success that took place _recently_ and is very _relevant_ to the new role for which they are interviewing, they establish themselves as one of the top candidates for the position.

Now It Is Your Turn:

Below, List the top successes that you have achieved throughout your career. Then, to the left, rank those items from 1 to 10 as most relevant to the new position that you will be interviewing for in the future. Please note, the ***recent and relevant*** successes that you choose to share in your next interview may change from interview to interview depending on the position that you are applying for in the moment. As a result, you will want to update these successes in preparation for each new interview.

My *Recent and Relevant* Successes

Rank   **Recent Successes That Are Relevant to the New Job**

_____   _____

_____   _____

_____   _____

_____   _____

_____   _____

_____   _____

_____   _____

_____   _____

_____   _____

_____   _____

_____   _____

_____   _____

_____   _____

_____   _____

_____   _____

_____   _____

KEY #7: FAILURE = LEARNING

—❧❧❧—

I t is human nature for people to take pause when asked about their failures. We much prefer to talk about our successes. Failure, for most people, is an indication of our inadequacies to accomplish a desired goal or objective. Most people feel that failure is an indication of weakness and vulnerability. Failure, in other words, is something that most candidates want to avoid like the plague when it comes to the interview process.

That is one of the reasons why so many candidates fail to effectively answer this question. When asked about a time they failed, most candidates share a weak story about something that went wrong earlier in their career and how there were countless extenuating circumstances that lead up to the failure. In other words, they do everything in their power to position the failure in such a way that you clearly believe it was not at all their fault. When I video record candidates and watch them answering this question, both their words and their physiology shift to a weak and anemic posture and tone. It often sounds something like this:

Interviewer: *"Can you tell me about a time that you failed?"*
Candidate: (eyes shift down and to the right, they make a strained facial expression, their shoulders hunch forward slightly) *"Hmmm. Well, I would not necessarily call it a failure* (long pause) *... but I guess*

a kind of failure that, uh, I've, you know, seen occur was a project we were working on two months ago. I was responsible for the project and no one ...(sigh) ... was reporting the numbers. Several of my peers and direct reports were not showing up at key meetings (sigh), *and uh,* (chuckle) *so I had to let the Executive Sponsor know what, you know, what was going on and he, he, he was not happy. We did accomplish a couple of the objectives but not nearly, um, like, you know, enough to satisfy the big wigs or whatever. I didn't get the direction I needed and no one spent time, you know, telling me what to do. Nothing I said seemed to matter to my direct reports and so it was just a bad project all around."* (head down and eyes looking at the paper in front of them)"

One of the greatest mishaps that occur during the answer to this question is that the candidate shares the story of their failure ... and then stops. They dance around the details and the story simply ends with the fact that they failed. It is such a missed opportunity!

First, like the weakness question, who has ever had a failure occur in their lives? The answer is *everyone*. All of us have had failures occur throughout our career at one time or another. This is why we have found that the first advanced strategy to answering the interview question surrounding your failure is an observational statement up front that sounds like this. *"Failure? Absolutely I have had times when I failed. You don't reach a level in your career that I have without having had a failure or two along the way."* By doing this, it instantly puts the interviewer in a state of mind to reflect, if even for a moment, on their own failures. When the interviewer considers the fact that they, too, have had a failure or two along the way, it generates an instant bond and connection between the interviewer and the candidate. They both have failed and the candidate will now show strength, self-awareness, and vulnerability by being willing to share one of their failures. This also creates instant interpersonal credibility for the candidate during the interview process.

Second, over ninety percent of the candidates I have worked with admit that they do not like the fact that they may have to talk about a failure during their interview. They often say it makes them feel weak and vulnerable. However, during my countless informal surveys of interviewers and applicants, one hundred percent admit that there were times when they learned more from their failures than from their successes. These two statements appear to be incongruent.

The biggest struggle that many candidates face when answering the failure question is that their response is only about the failure. In all of my work in recruiting over the past two decades, one thing is very clear. Interviewers know that we have all failed at one time or another in our careers. As a result, interviewers are less concerned with your failure, and more interested in what you *learned* from the failure. Therefore, candidates must gain a new perspective on what failure means to them in their career. You see, failure does not mean weakness. Failure = Learning.

Failure = Learning.
Interviewers are less concerned with the fact that you may have failed and more interested in what you have *Learned* from the failure.

Candidates who *nail* their answer to this question focus less on the fact that they had a failure, and more on articulating what they learned from the failure and how that learning applies to the new position for which they are interviewing. I also encourage candidate to pick a "real" failure. Not something that is insignificant. Rather, I encourage candidates to reference a real failure that was challenging and difficult but one that they truly learned from. By doing so, the candidate can speak with much more conviction and legitimate examples of what they learned throughout the challenge and how they can apply this learning to their new role.

I also encourage candidates to choose an example that is at least one to two years old. I do not recommend that you pick something that was twenty years ago (it actually looks weaker to some interviewers as it appears you have had no important responsibilities since that timeframe) nor do I recommend that you pick something that was within the last six months (it concerns many interviewers that you failed so recently and they begin to make too many assumptions of a likely failure in your new role.). Rather, I have found that what appears to be strongest in the interview is an example that is true and that reflects a little bit of distance between your current projects and initiatives and the project/initiatives that are associated with the failure. As a result, it is best to pick an example that is at least one to two years old.

Additionally, I have had candidates that ask me if the failure should be work related or if it would be acceptable to share a personal failure. While each candidate has to live by their own convictions, I never encourage personal examples in the professional interview as they rarely, if ever, play in your favor. Personal examples (especially when it comes to either failures or weaknesses) almost always turn the interviewer off from the candidate. Unless requested by the interviewer, always stick with professional examples. This is just one example of how a candidate may answer this important interview question.

Interviewer: *"Can you tell me about a time that you failed?"*
Candidate: (good eye contact) *"Failure? Absolutely. You do not reach a point in your career that I have without having had a failure or two along the way.* (speaking clearly and concisely) *Three years ago I was*

working on a project that required multiple stakeholders to be engaged and in alignment. I was the project owner and responsibility for success rested on my shoulders. However, key members of the project were often absent from critical calls and meetings. Because we needed their input, it slowed the entire process down and it took much longer for the team to gain agreement on even the simplest decisions. The project fell behind, our executive leaders were not happy, and we missed a key deadline. I had to stand in front of our sponsoring committee and acknowledge that we missed the first critical milestone. It was at that point that I admitted that this delay was purely my fault. As the project lead, I have to stand accountable regardless of the reasons for the delay. That was painful for me and I never wanted that to happen again. So, what I do now with every one of my projects is establish parameters of engagement for the team. Up front, we sign written agreements to hold one another accountable for being present. I establish clear ground rules and they are included in every meeting and on every agenda I publish. I also have accountability self-measures for each person that shows a "red, yellow, green" status so that each member reports their own engagement. Since that timeframe, every single project that I have been responsible for has been delivered on time and under budget. That failure three years ago was a tough one to experience but I sure learned from it and I believe I can bring that kind of productivity and accountability to this new position as well."

An advanced technique surrounding the answer to this question is to know that interviewers are less concerned with WHAT the failure was and more interested in what you LEARNED from the experience. Also, when you can demonstrate how you will leverage the learning you acquired from the failure and how you will use it to drive success in the new position, interviewers cannot help but be encouraged and impressed.

As a result, what you have essentially done is take your "mess" and make it your "message."

**The key to answering questions about your failures:
You must take your *"mess"* and make it your *"message."***

On video, the difference in the two approaches described in this chapter is very visually evident. The candidate who owns their failure and shares what they learned from it speaks with so much more confidence and clarity than any other candidate. This candidate tends to make more eye contact with the interviewer, their shoulders are up and back, and they are clearer and more descriptive in their speech. Hands down, this approach makes all the difference in the midst of an important interview. When you utilize the seventh key to crushing the interview (Failure = Learning), you will have *crushed* the interview question, *"tell me about a time when you failed."* You are ready now for the next advanced strategy to *nailing* the interview.

<u>**Now It Is Your Turn:**</u>
Below, List several of the failures you have experienced in your career. Next, outline what you learned from the failure and why it is relevant to the new position. In other words, how will you leverage these learnings to ensure success in your new role. Then, to the left, rank those items from 1 to 10 as most relevant to the role for which you are interviewing. Please note that the stories you select (Failures & Learnings) may change from interview to interview depending on the position that you are applying for in the moment. As a result, you will want to update these rankings in preparation for each new interview.

My Failures and What I *Learned*

Rank	Failure Examples	What I Learned & How It is Relevant

KEY #8:
HYPOTHETICALLY SPEAKING

—◦◦◦—

Today, most employers have discovered the power and importance of behavioral-based interviewing (as described in the chapter entitled *Behavioral-Based Interviewing* located earlier in this book). As a result, hypothetical questions have diminished as a percentage of the questions asked in most interviews today. The reason why hypothetical questions have diminished over time is the fact that employers have discovered that if a candidate is asked a behavioral-based question such as, *"What <u>HAVE</u> you done in the past in a particular situation,"* they will get an experience-based answer. However, if they ask a hypothetical question, *"What <u>WOULD</u> you do in a particular situation,"* the candidate can make up just about any answer that sounds reasonable – even if they have never actually experienced that particular situation in the past. Nonetheless, we find that hypothetical questions are still alive and well in the interviewing arena today.

Additionally, there are thousands of hypothetical questions that could be asked in an interview setting and a million variations as to how they are structured. As a result, I will simply select one form of a hypothetical question and provide you with an advanced strategy as to how to effectively answer this particular version of a hypothetical question. Just two examples of a hypothetical question include:

> **Interviewer:** *"What do you think you WOULD do if three of your team members entered your office and all resigned at the same time?"*
> **Interviewer:** *"Which would you select if you had to choose: To expand your office space as requested by your peers or use those budget dollars to develop an employee recognition program as requested by your direct reports?"*

For the purposes of this chapter, we will select the second hypothetical question above and review best practices for effectively answering this question in the interview. However, before I share the advanced strategies for *nailing* the answer to this question, I will share with you the key challenges candidates face when it comes to this type of hypothetical question in the interview.

The pitfall that so many candidates fall into when it comes to a hypothetical question is believing that there is a "right answer" to the question. As a result, they focus all their mental and emotional energy on deciding which option is correct. They start a mental debate with themselves over which answer is the right answer and this "mental debate" (the argument between the "file clerk" and the "construction worker with a bull horn" in their brain) is all clearly visible to the interviewer in the form of non-verbal communication (eyes looking up to the ceiling to search for the right answer, fidgeting fingers, eyes squinting as they search over the shoulder of the interviewer for the logical response, etc.). This "mental debate" is also often audible to the interviewer as some candidates begin a verbal debate with themselves. It often sounds like the following:

Interviewer: *"Which would you select if you had to choose: To expand your office space as requested by your peers or use those budget dollars to develop an employee recognition program as requested by your direct reports?"*

Candidate: (furrowed brows as they contemplate this challenge) *"Well, I guess I could expand the office space.but,* (pause) *uh,* (now eyes focused on the edge of the table as they struggle to think of all the nuances of each option) *that would not really solve the problem, would it? Hmmm. So, uhhhhh, maybe a recognition program would be better* (now smiling as they look out the window searching for clarity) *... but my peers may be unhappy with that decision and that could create tension in the office ... hmmmm??").* O.k. *Ummmmmm, this is a tough one* (looking up at the ceiling) *because I think there would be an advantage and disadvantage to both. Ok, if I have to choose,* (suddenly resolved and looks the interviewer straight in the eye because the "construction worker with a bullhorn" won out) *I would select the recognition program for my team."*

At this point, regardless of the candidate's answer, both their verbal and non-verbal queues provided the interviewer with insight into how that person responds to difficult challenges. Often interviewers make an automatic determination that this person is indecisive, unclear, and struggles with making a decision. Whether accurate or inaccurate, this verbal and non-verbal behavior in the interview can cause the interviewer to assume that this is how the candidate processes challenging questions on the job every day (unsure, struggle, indecisive, etc.).

The answer provided in the statement above is what we most often hear as an answer to this type of hypothetical question. The answer is typical, which is why it is so ineffective. As a candidate that wants to stand out from the crowd, this question is another opportunity for you to outshine the competition and really impress the interviewer.

You must respond to hypothetical questions with a behavioral-based answer

The first secret to effectively answering hypothetical questions is to respond with a behavioral-based answer. When applicable, articulate a similar decision that you have had to make in the past and demonstrate how you would answer this question in a similar manner as to how you HAVE made a challenging decision in the past. By referencing an historical event in your career (preferably recent), you demonstrate the fact that you are experienced in making challenging decisions and are up for the challenges of the new role. When you do this, you appear to be a far stronger candidate than those candidates who simply guess at what they believed to be a "right answer" to this hypothetical question and hope that they got their answer correct.

Additionally, the second secret to effectively answering a hypothetical question is to provide the interviewer with insight into _HOW_ you process your thoughts and make complex decisions (vs. WHAT you would select from the list of options). When the interviewer is asking a hypothetical question, most candidates believe that there must be a "right answer" and that if they are smart enough they will logically reason through all the possibilities and figure out the answer. They feel it is a "trick" question and a puzzle to be solved (like a Rubik's Cube) so they dive in and immediately work hard to solve the problem to demonstrate their intelligence in figuring out the "right answer."

The real challenge lies in the fact that it _is_ a trick question, but not in the way they think it is. In other words, there is a right answer to this question, it just so happens to not be any of the choices that are being offered in the question. Let me explain.

Another secret to effectively answering hypothetical questions lies within the fact that the option you choose is not what really matters to most interviewers. This is the perfect example of the old adage, "It's not so much WHAT you say, but HOW you say it." The secret to answering any hypothetical question is in pre-determining *HOW* you will answer a hypothetical question before you even walk into the interview. Some candidates may feel that they cannot prepare an answer for a question when they do not know what question is going to be asked. However, I have good news for you. Yes you can! The secret is to know the key fundamentals of *HOW* you process your thoughts when faced with a complex choice and then to state how you process your thoughts to make a decision with clarity and confidence.

When being asked a hypothetical question, the power of the "right answer" is not in WHAT option you choose, but rather in HOW you decide to choose it. The interviewer is usually less interested in you choosing option A or option B, and more interested in how you articulate your thought process in deciding option A or option B. Therefore, you can simply pre-determine what you will say when a hypothetical question is asked (regardless of the topic or choices). In other words, decide up front how you will articulate your thought process to make your selection. For example, often critical to making a key decision is gaining feedback and insight from your boss and other leaders you respect. Their advice and experience may help you to make a better decision. Also very important when making a decision is ensuring you are aligned with your boss and that they support your decision. The answer from candidates who utilize this advanced technique to answering hypothetical questions is so much stronger than those who try so desperately to ensure they choose the "right option."

Last, in addition to knowing the three or four key thought processes that you want to highlight when answering a hypothetical question, you also want to be sure that you share those thought processes with confidence and clarity. The way in which you share these thought processes should be in alignment with how you answer all of your interviewing questions. That is, leverage the power of the "Triumphant Twins" (confidence *and* humility). Be strong in your words, but not arrogant. Be clear in sharing your thought processes yet humble in your tone and demeanor. Here is a general example for what the best answer to any hypothetical question should sound like:

> **Interviewer**: *"Which would you select if you had to choose?: expand your office space as requested by your peers or use those budget dollars to develop an employee recognition program as requested by your direct reports?"*
>
> **Candidate**: *"Making a decision like this can often have a huge impact on my peers, my team, my boss, and the entire organization. The first thing I would want to do is ensure that I understand the concerns and issues of both my peers and my team members regarding these two very different requests. I also want to call upon my formal and informal mentors so that I can learn from their experience and coaching. Then, critical to this process, I want to share all that information with my boss to ensure we are in alignment and that my boss is bought into the decision that I make. Once I have done all these things, I will partner with my boss and make the decision that makes the most sense for all those involved. Without this process, it would be difficult, if not foolish, to make the decision without taking the proper steps because the decisions I make will have an impact on many people. Once this process is complete, however,*

I would make the final decision and clearly communicate the decision to all those impacted by it."

Notice that the above statement takes into consideration all the individuals who may be impacted by the outcome. The secret here is that the interviewer now has insight into <u>*HOW*</u> you will make important decisions on a regular basis. The typical candidate focuses on <u>WHAT</u> the right answer is. The *"Nailed It"* candidate (You) focuses on <u>HOW</u> to determine which option to choose. Do not get caught up in the minutia of a hypothetical question and get snared in the trap of thinking that there is a right answer. In fact, in most cases (with very few exceptions) there is not a right answer to a hypothetical interviewing question. There is, however, a right way to articulate the process you will utilize to answer the hypothetical question. The answer I provided above utilizes an advanced technique to answering this type of question. You will want to get clear on the specific decision making factors that you will reference in the interview process and leverage those terms when answering hypothetical inquiries. In addition to the best way to answer hypothetical questions, there are also best practices for preparing questions that you will ask the interviewers at the end of your interview. The questions that you ask your interviewer are a critical piece of the puzzle to absolutely *nailing* every single job interview you experience.

Now It Is Your Turn.

For your convenience, I have placed an area below for you to outline the decision-making factors that you will reference in the interview process (i.e. align with my boss, gather feedback from peers, etc.). Please note that the behavioral-based examples that you choose to share in your next interview may change from interview to interview depending on the position that you are applying for in the moment. As a result, you will want to update these examples in preparation for each new interview.

Process I Use To Make An Informed Decision	Behavioral-Based Example

KEY #9: FRONT LOAD

A t this point as a candidate, you have gone through the entire inter-view process and have now reached the end of your interview. You have been asked numerous questions and it is now time for the interviewer to hand over the reigns of the interview to you and allow you to ask all the questions. The interviewer now asks, *"Do you have any questions for me?"*

I am personally passionate about the question-asking portion of the interview. In fact, I find this particular part of the interviewing process absolutely fascinating. Through my research, I have found that effective questions at the end of the interview are often a key factor that separates one candidate from another.

There are two common traps that candidates get snared by in the ques-tion-asking portion of the interview. The first trap is a simple, easily recog-nizable pitfall. Unfortunately, countless candidates walk straight into this trap with a smile on their face and a skip in their step. Even after the interview has been completed, some candidates do not realize that they got caught in this trap and cannot figure out why they are not offered the position. They have fallen prey to the oldest interview trap in the book. "What is this trap?," you might ask. The trap that ensnares so many can-didates is the trap of having no questions at all.

It is common that I will have participants at my workshops say to me, *"But the interviewer really did answer all of the questions I had so what is wrong with not having any questions?"* Remember, the best indicator that an interviewer has of how you will perform tomorrow if they hire you, is how you are performing right now during the interview. When a candidate states they "have no questions," the interviewer (fair or unfair) immediately makes two assumptions as to why you have no questions.

The first immediate assumption is that you had not prepared adequately enough for the interview to even think of or pre-write a few questions. Needless to say, it is not the assumption you want the interviewer to make about you (especially as their final impression of you at the end of your interview).

The second major assumption that interviewers often make when a candidate has no questions is that you are not really interested in the position (either you do not like what you have heard, you would not enjoy working with the company, or you did not enjoy your conversation with the interviewer). These assumptions all take place within the span of about two seconds after you make your statement that you do not have any questions. It does not matter that their assumptions may be untrue, unfair, and completely inaccurate. The reality is that these types of assumptions are frequently made in the interview process. All of these assumptions are negative and all of them usually end in a negative outcome for you as the candidate. Few have survived the entrapment of not having any questions at the end of the interview.

It is important to note that interviewers typically view candidates who have well thought out, intelligent questions to ask at the end of the interview as more organized, more prepared, and more genuinely interested in acquiring the role. Not having well thought out questions in advance of the interview can be fatal to your chances to win the interview game and get that job or promotion that you have worked so hard to obtain.

As a result, many of my clients say to me, *"I would never fall into a trap like not having any questions at the end of the interview. In fact, I always have a few questions written down in preparation for the interview."*

Most candidates have heard the basic question-asking techniques of making sure you have a couple of questions to ask in the interview, doing your research so that you can ask intelligent questions, and making sure you interview the company during this process to make sure they are the right company for you as well. Because of this common knowledge, almost every candidate that we speak to begins to formulate the questions they plan to ask at the close of the interview. When candidates have pre-thought out questions, they usually sound like the following:

Interviewer: *"I have asked you a lot of questions. Do you have any questions for me?"*

Typical Candidate: *"A question that I have is:*
With offices in Cincinnati and Orlando, will I have the opportunity to lead team members located at both offices?"

Typical Candidate: *"A question that I have is:*
Stepping into the VP role of this organization, how many Board Members are there and how often will I get to present to the Board?"

Typical Candidate: *"A question that I have is:*
What challenges in culture do you face within your organization and what is the organization doing to improve the culture?"

The above questions demonstrate the second most common trap that candidates fall into when preparing their questions for the end of the interview. You may notice that all of these questions are very well thought-out, intelligent questions that the candidate writes down and brings with them to the interview. You will also notice that each of these questions is designed to learn about the company and/or the position. These two things combined are the primary reasons why they lead to the second most common trap in the question-asking segment of the interview. This trap is not only common, it is massive and it is difficult to free yourself from it. The trap is preparing well articulated interview questions that are designed for you to **_get_** information. Let me explain further why this is a trap.

Typical interviewing candidates for any given position will ask good, intelligent questions to **_get_** information. **_Nailed It_** interviewing candidates, on the other hand, never ask questions to **_get_** information. **_Nailed It_** interviewing candidates ask advanced interviewing questions that are designed to **_give_** information. The easiest way to remember this formula is simple:

Typical candidates ask questions to _GET_ information.
Nailed It candidates ask questions to _GIVE_ information.

Nailed It candidates ask questions to **_GIVE_** information. I call this process "front loading." Candidates simply "front load" their question with important stats and data regarding their previous experiences that further support the fact that they are an applicable candidate for the job. They utilize the question-asking portion of the interview to reinforce all their key experiences and strengths. Candidates who leverage our advanced interviewing skills understand the fact that the interview is won by *nailing* all areas of the interview. The question asking portion of the interview is no exception.

As a result, candidates who utilize the "front loading" strategy start their questions off with <u>key facts</u> that reinforce what the interviewer is looking for in candidates for this particular position. The back half of their question remains the same as other typical candidates. In other words, the questions they ultimately ask are very well thought out, intelligent question as well. However, advanced interviewers will "front load" their question with facts and/or data that tell a story and make a powerful statement about their accomplishments and abilities as a candidate. This is an example of a "front loaded" question.

> **<u>Interviewer</u>**: *"I have asked you a lot of questions. Do you have any questions for me?"*
> **<u>Candidate utilizing the "Front Loading" question-asking strategy</u>**: *"Yes, thank you. I have a few questions. First, in my current role, I have had the privilege of directing leadership teams in seven different cities and two different time zones, with 97% of my 68 team members consistently performing at or above expectations for a period of over three years. I am curious that with you having offices in Cincinnati and Orlando, will I have the opportunity to lead team members located at both offices?"*

Notice the difference in tone and professionalism that is conveyed by this type of frame up. Candidates who utilize the "front loading" question-asking technique find that with each successive question, they can feel "The Stacking Effect" at work in this section of the interviewing process (more so here than in any other area of the interview). This technique is so powerful and so rarely used by typical candidates that when questions are framed to **GIVE** information to interviewers rather than to simply **GET** information, candidates appear to be more professional, more intelligent, and interviewers often state that they feel the candidate is a better "fit" for their organization.

Interviewers I have worked with over the past two decades share with me that candidates who utilize this approach provide a much richer end-of-interview experience and it quickly catapults them to the top of the candidate list. Most candidates ask really good, intelligent questions. Actually, that is the problem. Why? Because that is what everyone does! Therefore, the candidate who asks those typical, intelligent questions do not stand out from the rest of the candidates interviewing for the role. However, when candidates frame up each of their questions by **GIVING** information that is pertinent to the role they are interviewing for ("front loading"), it is so powerful for the interviewers that they feel many similar experienced and educated candidates do not even come close to these candidates as being most applicable for the role. When "front loading" your questions, remember to keep your facts straight, keep it numbers-based (dollars, percentages, etc.) and keep the information relevant to the role. When "front loading," there are two important things to note when utilizing this strategy.

First, candidates who utilize these advanced techniques understand that the facts you utilize when "front loading" your questions must be relevant to the role in order to maximize their impact. For example, the "front loading" of data in the above interview example has no impact if it does not apply to the position for which you are interviewing. In other words, there is less value in GIVING the information that you "directed leadership teams in seven different cities" if the position you are applying for does not require that experience. In fact, this may be an example of overusing the "front loading" technique. Some candidates oversell their experiences and the interviewer feels they are over-qualified for this particular position. In other words, they "front loaded" too much information, which causes them to fall on their face in the interview. Remember, "front loading" is like a fine ingredient in a great recipe. You do not want to over spice it. Just a little bit (two to three questions) is enough. Balance is required when utilizing this strategy.

Second, candidates who utilize this advanced technique understand that the information they are sharing is more important than the answers they receive. In other words, because the question-asking section is still part of the interview, the information a candidate <u>provides</u> is MORE important than the answers they <u>receive</u> from the interviewer. While both are important and both do matter, your provision of information supersedes your need to get a question answered. In other words, if you *nail* the question-asking portion of the interview by "front loading" with key experiences packed with statistics that deliver a punch, you will impact the interviewer so powerfully that you will (either now or in the very near future) get all your questions answered because you will more likely find yourself being offered the position.

Conversely, typical candidates who utilize standard question-asking techniques that everyone else uses (simply good, intelligent questions) tend to forget the fact that during the question-asking portion of the interview they are still being interviewed. I have video record countless clients that I work with (ranging from Senior Professionals and NFL Football Prospects to graduating college seniors and middle managers of large corporations) and the vast majority of these candidates ask really good, intelligent questions that are designed solely to **GET** information. Therefore, they miss yet another opportunity to set themselves apart from all the other equally qualified candidates by "front loading" their question with information that can further indicate that they are the most qualified candidate for the position. In fact, it is very evident on video that when candidates finally reach the question-asking portion of the interview, they start to relax.

When the candidate finally reaches the portion of the interview where they get to ask questions, their physiology changes. In their mind, the interview is primarily over. They now get to become the interviewer, which feels more empowering. When watching a candidate's video-recorded interview, you can physically see the candidates relax their posture, take a deep breath, and let down their guard. The interviewer, of course, never tells the candidate that their behavior has shifted into a more casual posture and that the candidate is starting to become a little bit too relaxed in their tone and body language. The candidate is often doing this even though the interviewer, in the question asking portion of the interview, is still paying a great deal of attention to the candidate and continuing to assess their behavior and tone. The candidate is still being interviewed but temporarily forgets that fact when they are asking all the questions. It is so unfortunate because it is typical behavior for many candidates. It is the standard "ho hum" approach to this portion of the interview. Interviewers have seen it all before and these candidates look and sound just like everyone else does in the question-asking section of the interview. It is so devastating to their chances of winning the interview because that is what everyone else does. You are not everyone else. You are ready to be an advanced interviewer and the "front loading" technique will separate you from the rest of the pack.

To reinforce this point, I will share two additional examples utilizing the sample questions I provided earlier. You saw what typical questions look like in the interview process. Let's compare those same sample questions with questions that are asked utilizing the "front loading" technique. Here is the first example:

Interviewer: *"I have asked you a lot of questions. Do you have any questions for me?"*

Typical Candidate: *"A question that I have is:*

Stepping into the VP role of this organization, how many Board Members are there and how often will I present to the Board?"

Candidate utilizing the Front Loading question-asking strategy:

"When I was with my previous corporation, I had the opportunity to work very closely with the Board of Directors and provided monthly presentations to their team with 78% of my proposals being accepted by the board. Stepping into the VP role with your organization, how many Board Members are there and how often will I get to present to the Board?"

A second comparison includes the following example:

Interviewer: *"I have asked you a lot of questions. Do you have any questions for me?"*

Typical Candidate: *"A question that I have is:*
What challenges in culture do you face within your organization and what is the organization doing to improve the culture?"

Candidate utilizing the Front Loading question-asking strategy:

"In my last position, I was charged with leading an effort to change and improve the culture of our workplace. I managed a team of 4 VP's, 7 Sr. Directors and 14 Key Managers tasked with assessing our culture, interviewing over 70 leaders and 200 employees, and establishing plans to positively shift our culture to create greater employee engagement and improve productivity. Our CEO today considers it the greatest achievement we have had in our organization in over 20 years. What challenges in culture do you face within your organization and what is the organization doing to improve the culture?"

Notice that with the information that is provided before each question, it sends the interviewer on a mental journey. This mental journey simply helps them to see you stepping into this position and immediately having a positive and powerful impact on their organization. When you "front load" your questions with facts, data and information tied to relevant expectations for the position for which you are applying, it further solidifies you as a top candidate for the role. This technique also gives you the platform to ensure that all your best examples, stories, and experiences are articulated during this portion of the interview (especially if the interviewer has not asked about those experiences and accomplishments earlier in the process). In other words, if you have not yet had a chance to share a key experience or major accomplishment that you wanted them to know about you, the question-asking segment of the interview is the perfect place to "front load" your questions with this information.

The more savvy you become in the interview process, the quicker you will find yourself coming up with these "front loaded" statements that end with a key question. "Front Loading" is simple, practical, and powerful. Questions are often the key to winning the interview. *Nail* this technique, and you are well on your way to an offer letter for the position you have been working toward your whole career!

Now It Is Your Turn:

List below the key stats or data from previous accomplishments that you want to share during the question-asking portion of the interview (this process is called "front loading"). Then, write the question that you will ask the interviewer based on the information you shared. Please note that the questions and date that you choose to share in your next interview may change from interview to interview depending on the position that you are applying for in the moment. As a result, you will want to update these questions and the data you provide in preparation for each new interview.

My "Front Loaded" Questions For The Interview

Information/Stats/Data/Numbers I will use to "Front Load" my 1st question:

_____

_____

The First Question I Will Ask:

_____

_____

Information/Stats/Data/Numbers I will use to "Front Load" my 2nd question:

_____

_____

The Second Question I Will Ask:

_____

_____

Information/Stats/Data/Numbers I will use to "Front Load" my 3rd question:

_____

_____

The Third Question I Will Ask:

_____

_____

Information/Stats/Data/Numbers I will use to "Front Load" my 4ᵗʰ question:

_____

_____

The Fourth Question I Will Ask:

_____

Information/Stats/Data/Numbers I will use to "Front Load" my 5ᵗʰ question:

_____

The Fifth Question I Will Ask:

_____

KEY #10: MOST & MIGHT

—⌘—

You have made it through the interview. Things seem to be going well. The interviewers seem to be smiling a lot and nodding frequently. That is a good sign, right? You have asked a few great "front loaded" questions and they have answered them willingly. Everything seems to be going well and it is time for the interview to come to a close. They stand up. You stand up. They shake your hand and you smile. You are at the finish line and all you have to do is break that tape and you will have successfully completed the race. Suddenly, you are feeling a stirring in your gut and a trembling on your lips. You have given a strong interview but you hear the "construction worker with the bullhorn" shouting loudly in his megaphone, *"You heard me. We are on a tight deadline here so ask them now!!"* You find you cannot hold it back any longer. Your lips start to move and before you can think twice about it, you blurt it out. It is a question. It is a simple little question. It almost seems intuitive. Harmless really. You start to reason, *"Why not ask it? It is a fair question, after all."* The words roll off your tongue and the question is asked, *"What are next steps and when will I hear back from you?"*

Sounds innocent enough, doesn't it? After all, that is what most people ask at the end of an interview, right? The answer, as you know, is yes. And once again, that is the problem with this question. In fact, this question is the same basic question that everyone asks at the end of the interview. You will even find that they teach this to high school students when they are applying for their first job at a fast food joint. That is why it is such a devastating question for you to ask at the end of your interview. It is disastrous for two reasons.

First, this question is now the final question of your list of great questions that you have asked. The last great "front loaded" question that you asked (and that they were impressed by as discussed in the previous chapter) is no longer their final impression. Rather, their final impression of you is now the question that all the other "typical" candidates ask during the interview. You have taken the interview, in this single moment, from *"wow, this person is incredibly sharp"* to *"hmmm, sounds just like all the other average applicants that we have talked to today."* You are now lumped in with all the other average candidates who are good people but will not be offered the position. Many candidates find themselves running this 26.2 mile marathon we call the interview only to trip at the finish line! As an advanced interviewer, you want your final question to leave them with a "wow" not a "whimper."

You want to close your interview with a "wow" not a "whimper."

Secondly, ending the interview with asking the question, *"When will I hear back from you?"* is destructive because if you really pay attention, you will notice that it makes the candidate sound desperate. Remember, this question is <u>not</u> a bad question. It is just a "typical" question, which makes a great candidate suddenly appear average. If a candidate has to ask, *"What are next steps and when will I hear back from you?,"* then they have not captivated their audience and led with such great confidence that the interviewer wants (actually needs) to share with you what next steps will be because they hope to speak with you again soon. After viewing thousands of hours of interviewing videos, the reality is that almost all interviewers (whether impressed or not impressed with the candidates) will share this information anyway at the end of the interview. However, if the candidate feels the need to ask it, it causes the candidate to appear needy, vulnerable, and (if you saw how it appears on video) desperate.

Furthermore, what I find most humorous about this question is that almost every person interviewing for a job ALREADY knows the answer. Most professional candidates already know what the interview process typically looks like and how long it will be before they hear back from the interviewers. During my workshops, I noticed that from entry-level professionals to senior executives, almost everyone asks this question at the close of the interview. However, in one of my interviewing workshops at a Fortune 50 company, I asked an entire group of senior executives this question, *"What are next steps and when would you typically hear back from an interviewer?"* Without exception and without hesitation, they all shouted out the answers. Every person in the room had interviewed others before and were very familiar with the interviewing process. Each person could outline the fact that, *"It takes a few weeks to complete the interviews, then they will select the top two or three candidates for a second interview, and last they will offer the position and notify the rest of the candidates."* While there are few exceptions, the vast majority of interviewers follow this same process. As a result, 95% of the candidates asking the typical question, *"What are next steps and when will I hear back from you?,"* already know the answer! That is why this is such a junior-level question and should be reserved for only the least experienced candidates.

There are additional final questions that people often ask in an interview that are fatal to their chances for securing the position. One of the worst final questions that candidates can ask (I call it the "death trap"), is *"How did I do?"* So many great candidates have fallen into this trap and most do not survive its fatal blows. Candidates do not realize that when they ask this question, it causes them to look very inexperienced regardless of what level position they are applying for in the organization. They look junior in their role, even if they have been in an executive leadership position for over a decade. On video, the candidate appears to have a low self-esteem when asking this question. They wince and squint and smile nervously as they await the response. The candidate appears to not be very self-aware and they do not realize that asking this question assumes they were playing a "role" on a theatrical stage ("Ta Dah! ... So, how did I do?"). The interviewer often wanders if this person was acting the whole time and would like some feedback on their stage performance so that they can do better next time. It is a self-serving question (its all about me, after all) and interviewers report that they feel like they are having to tell a high school student in the school choir (who cannot carry a tune in a bushel basket) that they did 'just fine' during their singing tryouts for the school musical (even though they will recommend them only as a stage hand when they discuss this person's performance with others). Even if the candidate had a strong interview, they trip at the finish line when asking this question.

When we asked candidates why they even asked this question, they often transparently admitted that they needed reassurance that they did well. They do not want to go home and have to say to loved ones and friends, *"I'm not sure how it went."* As a result, they are seeking psychological relief from wandering what the interviewers truly felt about them as a candidate. Unknowingly, they are actually negatively shifting how the interviewers feels about them as a candidate by their asking this ineffective question.

Ironically, it is not uncommon that up until that point, they were considered a possible candidate and it was THAT very question alone that left the interviewers wandering, *"Maybe they are not as strong and confident as we thought if they need our approval for their interview."* Additionally (right, wrong or indifferent and fair or unfair), the truth is that interviewers report that they almost NEVER tell you the truth anyway in that moment because they feel like they are being put on the spot and do not like to give bad news if the interview was worthy of a "bad report." In other words, they are NOT going to tell you the full truth anyway so do not even bother to ask this question. Are there exceptions? Very few. But not enough to take the risk of asking such a risky question. It has the likelihood of making you look vulnerable and weak. In fact, I call it the "blankee" question.

When my son, Cole, was two years old, he was a major "blankee" baby. He loved his blankee and he carried it with him everywhere he went. There were times when he would be bold and adventurous and leave his blankee in the other room, but the moment he was scared or sad, he would instantly run to his "blankee" to receive solice and comfort. When watching the video of a candidate who asked the question, *"How did I do?,"* they often (without even realizing it) look like a small child who needs their favorite blankee to comfort them. It sounds like this to the interviewer: *"Please mister interviewer, Sir. Please tell me something good so I can feel good about myself again."* The interviewer will share a couple of mostly positive comments (regardless of whether they felt you were a strong candidate or not) and will not be able to articulate exactly why but they often tell us that they felt like the interview ended on a flat note. That is *NOT* how advanced interviewers want to end an interview. We call this question the "death trap" for a reason, and the pathway to the position you desire most is cluttered with the carnage of candidates who have asked this question in their interview.

There is another final question asked at the end of the interview that has equally devastating consequences. At face value, it also sounds like a "fair" question. However, when asked, it usually ends in a last ditch effort for the candidate to squeeze in their final "two cents worth" about why they are the best applicant for the position.

Not having done their research on the psychology behind interviewing, job seekers often feel that this question is a logical question for which to end the interview (and it never is). The question candidates often ask at the end of the interview is, *"What are the key attributes that you are looking for in candidates for this position?"* The problem with this question is the fact that to the interviewer, it sounds like a desperate plea to find out what else the interviewer needs to hear so that the candidate can spit it all out in twenty seconds or less during the final closing moments of the interview.

To many interviewers, it also sounds like you are willing to simply say whatever it is that they want to hear. Remember, this is the last question of the interview. They know that anything they articulate to you as important elements for the position that they have not heard from you yet, you are simply going to reply with the statement that indicates that you now magically have all those qualities. In other words, to the experienced interviewer, they have found that if they answer this question by truthfully stating, *"I was hoping to hear more about your ability to manage people as well as your ability to work with people at all levels of the organization,"* that the applicant will simply state *"Great because I can manage people very well and I always work well with people at all levels of the organization."* The candidate may change their words around a little bit but in reality, they almost always simply spit back as quickly as they can (since it is the end of the interview and the interviewer is looking at her watch quite frequently) the exact attributes the interviewer just stated. With one minute remaining before the interview is over, the interviewer states that they were looking for a motivated leader and what they hear from the applicant is, *"I've got good news – You need a motivated leader and I just happen to be a motivated leader"* (tah dah!). Even though the job seeker gave no verbal or non-verbal cues throughout the entire interview that they are motivated, they still believe it is important for them to say the words. The problem is it rarely, if ever, works.

Interviewers are not not impressed with last ditch efforts to share as many attributes as a candidate can think of to demonstrate that they are exactly the type of candidate the interviewer has been searching for all along. Interviewers also find themselves, conversely, very unimpressed with the fact that the candidate even considered using this junior-level approach.

Remember, behavioral-based interviewing is not just the interviewer asking questions about what you HAVE done in your past vs. what you MIGHT do if you had the position. Behavioral-based interviewing is also the interviewer noticing your verbal and non-verbal behavior and, without any other means to do so, predict what you will do tomorrow based on how you behave today in the interview. If you ask this question in the interview and respond by simply telling the interviewer everything they wanted to hear, an automatic assumption is made that tomorrow you are going to do the same thing in their important meetings if they hire you. The best predictor of how someone will perform on the job tomorrow is how they are behaving in the interview in this moment. Aside from the recommendations of other leaders and team members, the only thing the interviewer can use to predict your future behavior is how you are behaving in this moment during the interview.

That is why so many internal candidates who apply for a promotion within their current organization go into the interview with the testimonials of several leaders only to find that they do not get the job. These candidates perform well on the job (and, as a result, receive high accolades and recommendations from their boss and peers). However, they answer questions shyly or ask poor questions and the interviewer wonders, *"Is this the person everyone says is so awesome? I do not get it. This candidate's examples are dated, their answers are unclear, and the questions they asked were not very impressive. They have accomplished some great things in their career but I just do not think they are the right 'fit' for our department."* Regardless of the great recommendations of others, they often do not get hired because the interviewer could not see them holding this position given their behavior in the interview (statements they made, non-verbals and vocal tone, and the poor questions they asked). The interview is the best prediction interviewers have for determining how the candidate will perform tomorrow and a candidate's poor performance in the interview can often overshadow their glowing endorsements. It is sad. Mostly it is unfair. Nonetheless, it is true and it happens all the time. *"What then,"* you wonder, *"should I ask as my final question of the interview?"* There is a much better way to close the interview on a positive note by asking a final question that is extremely effective. This final question is what I call the "Closing Question."

The Power of the "Closing Question":

Would you agree that it would be nice if interviewers would simply close the interview by declaring all the things they liked most about you as a candidate? Would you agree that doing so would not only be inspiring to you as a candidate but also remove the stress of wandering what type of impression you left with the interviewer? That is exactly what the "Closing

Question" does for you. This question does all of those things as well as leaves your interviewer remembering all your greatest attributes. Do not close the interview with a "whimper." Close the interview with a "wow!" The "Closing Question" helps you to do exactly that.

You want to close your interview on a high note. It is important that your interviewers walk away from their conversation with you having a sense that you, by far, are the strongest candidate. One of the best ways to do this is to end on a powerful question that demonstrates humble confidence *and* that leaves them remembering your greatest qualities. Far more powerful than <u>you</u> stating your best attributes (which is a trap that many candidates fall into) is to have <u>the interviewer</u> state your best attributes in their own words. The "Closing Question" is simple yet it is very powerful and extremely effective.

The "Closing Question" (your final question at the end of the interview) must be spoken clearly yet humbly. As with all questions & statements in an interview, you want to be both confident and humble. If you ask any question too confidently, it sounds arrogant and can back fire. In fact, of all the interviewing tips, techniques, statements, and questions that I recommend in this book, this is the ONLY one that I'm going to encourage you to memorize *word-for-word*. This final closing question in the interview sounds like this:

Interviewer: *"Do you have any final questions before we close?"*
Candidate: *"I do have one final question. We have had a great conversation today. You have seen my resume and you have heard about many of my skills, experiences and abilities".* (**"Closing Question"**) *"Of all the things you have seen and heard today, what gives you the **MOST** confidence that I **MIGHT** be applicable for this position?"*

As a "Closing Question" to the entire interview, this particular question must be asked precisely as written. In fact, I encourage candidates to slow down a little bit when asking this question. The tone should be conversational and the candidate should be humble in their approach. Note that two things are emphasized in this question.

First, this final question establishes the fact that you are simply inquiring as to what gives the interviewer the "**most** confidence." Framed this way, this question tee's up the interviewer to simply share their highlights of what they find most compelling about the candidate's skills and experiences.

Second, this question establishes the fact that you humbly acknowledge that you **might** be applicable for the role. Note that this question is asking if you *ARE* applicable and not if you are the BEST candidate for the position. Rather, you are savvy enough not to make the fatal mistake of assuming you have got the job. That would (and often does) sound arrogant. This final question is asked from a humble position and, for that reason, the interviewer is more open and willing to answer the question.

The 10th Key To Crushing The Interview is *MOST* And *MIGHT* ("What gives you the *MOST* confidence that I *MIGHT* be applicable for this position?")

What I love most about this final "Closing Question" is that it sets up the interviewer to close the interview by stating in their own words the top two to three things they like most about you as a candidate. Inexperienced candidates often find themselves summarizing all their own best attributes at the end of their interview. It often sounds like the below example.

Interviewer: *"Do you have any final questions?"*

Typical Candidate: *"No, I just want you to know that I am a hard worker, I have really strong communication skills, and I will do everything I can to excel at this position."*

However, as an advanced interviewer, you ask the "Closing Question" and the interviewer will summarize your best attributes for you in *their* own words! Advanced interviewers who effectively utilize the "Closing Question" sound like this:

Candidate: *"I have one final question. We have had a great conversation today. You have seen my resume and you have heard about many of my skills, experiences and abilities. Of all the things you have seen and heard today, what gives you the **most** confidence that I **might** be applicable for this position?"*

Interviewer: *"I think what gives me confidence that you might be applicable for this position is your ability to communicate well with people at all levels of the organization. I also see that you have accomplished many things in your career, which indicates to me that you know how to drive for results. Last, I have seen that you can really develop a team well and that will be important for the leader who steps into this role."*

Candidate: *"Thank you."* (**Note: Do not continue talking at this point. Let the interviewer simply bring the interview to a natural close).

When the interviewer closes the interview by stating, in their own words, the top two to three attributes they like most about you as a candidate, it has a very profound impact on your interview.

First, if you share your own top attributes in your own words, they will forget it. However, if *they* say your top attributes in *their* own words, they are much more likely to remember it.

The second (and perhaps most powerful) reason why this approach is so effective is the fact that the words they speak (regarding your top attributes as a candidate) will literally be the last words spoken in your interview. As a result, your interview closes with the interviewer declaring for themselves the top two to three reasons why you are <u>applicable</u> for this position! Interviewers often remember *most* what is spoken *last*. The fact that they just said with their own words your top qualities, they tend to remember those things more than almost any other element from your interview.

Why is this called the "Closing Question?" There are a couple of reasons for the name. First, it is purposefully designed to literally <u>close</u> the interview and bring all interviewing conversations to an end. By design, I encourage candidates to make this literally the last dialogue they will have in the interview. Other than shaking hands and thanking them for the opportunity to interview for this position, the interviewer's answer to this question should be the last interviewing words spoken. This allows the interview to end on a very positive note and ensures that your top two to three attributes are the last words the interviewer has heard in your conversation (which further ensures they will remember it). When the last words spoken in your interview are the interviewer's justification as to why you are an applicable candidate for this position, it plays very heavily in your favor.

The second reason it is called the "Closing Question" is because we are leveraging a very powerful technique that is used in the sales industry across the globe. When a sales person is speaking to a client (whether it be a CEO working on a merger, a VP negotiating a contract with a multi-billion dollar client, or a consultant selling their services to an organization), they will often reach a point at the end of the conversation where they will ask for the sale. This "asking for the sale" takes on many forms, but generally sounds like one of the following examples.

> **CEO Example**: *"If we decide to shake hands on this merger today, which office do you prefer? The one on the top floor east corner facing the city or the one on the top floor west corner facing the river?"*
>
> **VP Example**: *"Now that I have shared my proposal with you today, which options will work best for your organization?"*
>
> **Consulting Example**: *"Of all the programs we are discussing today, which ones do you feel best meet the needs of your organization?"*

In all three cases, you will notice that by simply offering an answer to any of these questions above puts the individual in a position of actually making the decision to move forward with your proposal. In other words, with regards too the CEO Merger Example above, if the client says, *"I prefer the east view of the city,"* they are already moving toward a "yes" to your proposal (or, at the very least, seeing themselves sitting on the top floor east side office overlooking the city, which puts them one step closer to a "yes."). As a result, the "Closing Question" in the interview moves the interviewer closer to saying "yes" to you as a candidate. In the same way this works in business and sales meetings, it also works in the interview process.

When asked humbly and not presumptuously, this question presupposes that the interviewer has seen something in your interview that **might** cause you to be **applicable** for the position. The interviewer finds themselves answering the question and, without realizing it, they start selling themselves on the possibility of you being hired for the role. In fact, in order to answer the question, they often begin to visualize you in the position. When they do that, it provides them with a glimpse of what it would be like to hire you for this position. It is a very powerful final interviewing technique because you are successfully able to get them to tell you why you are an viable candidate for the role (and, at the least, a candidate that is worthy of the next level in the interviewing process.).

We also encourage candidates to end on this question and not to go into further questions at the end of the interview. You essentially leave the interviewer with the image of you sitting in the office where this position resides. They have stated your best attributes *in their own words*. This is why CEO's, Sr. Executives, and Leaders across the country are now utilizing my "Closing Question" strategy in board meetings, sales calls, and other important conversations. Bottom line ... it flat out WORKS! In fact, here is what my personal research unveiled about the "Closing Question."

Over 80% of interviewers state that following the interview, they either call or walk into the office of the other panel members who recently interviewed the same candidate and calibrate personal notes & experiences. Over 60% tell me that this process happens immediately after the candidate walks out of the office. As a result, they often share the things they remember most from your interview. When you end the interview with this "Closing Question," you are literally arming the interviewer with the information they are about to share with others in their calibration meeting regarding your applicability for the position. By sharing with you what "gives them the *most* confidence that you *might* be applicable for this position," the two to three elements are the **first** things they share when other panel members ask them, *"What did you think about this candidate?"*

Because they, themselves, spoke these attributes out loud in your interview, they are much more bought into the fact that they are your key strengths. Equally powerful, they never really summarized the key strengths of the other candidates who interviewed for the role. The other candidates' final question was, *"So what are next steps and when should I plan on hearing back from you?"* As a result, the interviewers have to dig deep through their notes to remember the other candidates' best attributes. But, for some reason (wink, wink), your top two to three attributes roll right off their tongue. You have essentially helped them sell themselves on you as a candidate and already they begin to visualize you in the role. If you have effectively established "The Stacking Effect" by answering all your other interview questions equally well (utilizing the advanced strategies we have outlined in this book), you will have secured "top billing" as their strongest candidate for this position.

A few more things I want to encourage you to do once you have asked this final "Closing Question." Remember, the sole purpose for asking this question is to end the conversation with the interviewer telling you the top two to three things they like most about you as a candidate. It is very powerful. However, I must warn you. There are a few traps that some candidates fall into after asking the "Closing Question." Make sure you avoid the following traps at all cost.

Trap #1: Not asking the "Closing Question" word-for-word

The first trap that candidates fall into is ***not*** asking this question <u>word-for-word</u>. In fact, this is not only the first trap, it is also the largest and most deadly trap. Why? The "Closing Question" is designed to be asked confidently (after all, you are asking for their feedback) yet humbly (to garner a response, it is important not to be too forward when asking this question). As I work with clients that are interviewing for a key position, I have discovered that some job seekers at almost every professional and executive level think that, without practice and memorization of this "Closing Question," they will be able to remember it when the end of the interview roles around. The reason why we encourage candidates (with this question only) to memorize the question <u>*word-for-word*</u> is that derivatives of this question can (and often do) sound incredibly arrogant and have the opposite effect that the question is intended to elicit.

For example, I have heard candidates who did not memorize the "Closing Question" like they were supposed to, ask this question in the following inaccurate (if not fatal) ways:

Bad Example 1: *"We have talked a lot today and you have seen my resume. What gives you confidence that I <u>am</u> the best candidate for this position?"*
(oops).

Bad Example 2: *"You have seen my resume and we have gone through this lengthy interview. What gives you the most confidence that I <u>should get</u> this position?"*
(oops)

Bad Example 3: *"After everything you have seen and heard, why do you think I might be the best one you have interviewed?"*
(oops)

Interviewer: (In all three examples, the interviewer will most likely reply with the following statement). *"We are not sure yet if you are the best candidate because we have many more candidates to interview."*

These derivatives of the "Closing Question" actually sound arrogant and closes your interview on a sour note for both you and the interviewer. In fact, these derivatives of your final interviewing question may very well negate any/all positive elements that you incorporated throughout your interview. It is the last experience they will remember and it is the first thing they will share with other panel members when they debrief after your interview. Avoid the trap of going "off script" when asking the "Closing Question."

Trap #2: Continuing to talk after the "Closing Question" has been answered

The second trap that candidates fall into when asking their "Closing Question" is the temptation to *keep talking*. Some candidates get caught up in the moment and they feel so good about the interviewer complimenting them that they do not want it to end. As a result, they say something like, *"Well, thank you! I love working with people as you mention and I do enjoy developing leaders. Just last week I was working with a leader that was struggling and I .... blah, blah, blah."*

The candidate takes the interview from ending on this incredibly high note to pulling the interviewers back into more dialogue. The interview, then, ends on a flat note. Do not fall into this trap! In fact, I tell my clients that once they have asked this final question, they must do one thing and one thing only. Shut Up! Shhhhh ... remain silent and do not continue to speak when they are finished. Listen with gratitude and humility. Once the interviewer has shared their top two to three reasons that give them the MOST confidence that you MIGHT be applicable for this position, you have permission to say only two words, which are *"Thank you."* Why? Because anything else will distract them from remembering the two to three reasons why they have confidence in your applicability in the first place.

Trap #3: Asking another question following the "Closing Question"

The third trap that job seekers fall into when asking their "Closing Question" is asking another question when they are finished. Once again, you want no distractors once you have asked this final interview question.

Your goal should be to get out of the interview quickly so they can talk to other interviewing panel members regarding your top two to three applicable attributes for the position. However, some candidates find that they cannot help themselves and must ask just *one* more question (sigh). They find themselves asking things like, *"why do you think that attribute is so important to you?"* or *"Do you also like the fact that I have great negotiation skills?"* or *"I also feel that my ability to manage others is a trait that will help me stand out above the crowd, don't you?"*

In addition to these questions, some candidates may also find themselves asking the questions I mentioned earlier in this chapter. Some of those questions include, *"When should I expect to hear back from you?"* or *"What are next steps in the process?"* Remember, these are *not bad* questions. They are just *weak* questions and they cause the interview to end on a flat note.

Interviewers must find great candidates for the position they are trying to fill. If you interviewed well, they are going to WANT to tell you when you will hear back from them and what the next steps will be in the process. Why? Because they have spent too much time and money to let an amazing candidate like you slip away. In fact, if you use all the advanced interviewing techniques I have shared with you in this book, you will find interviewers not only telling you what happens next without you needing to ask for that information, you will find (on occasion) interviewers who will immediately ask you back for a second interview. We also have countless reports of interviewers offering our candidates the job right there on the spot! Why? Because it is too expensive and time consuming to find the right person for the job and it is too risky to let the best candidate for the job slip away.

If you interview well, they would be crazy to let you walk out the door and have some other organization discover your talent and hire you before they get the chance. You want to interview so incredibly well that the interviewers quickly come to the conclusion that if they let you walk out the door, they will have blown a perfect opportunity for themselves as an interviewer, for the boss you will report to, for the department you will be working in, and for the organization overall. Hiring a weak candidate is too painful and too expensive to replace. They need the best candidate. When you utilize these advanced interviewing techniques, you will find interviewers who are anxious to get you back for next-level interviews. Some may even offer you the job on the spot!

The "Closing Question" separates candidates from all the rest of the competition and arms the interviewer with your best attributes spoken in their own words. Because their words were the last words spoken in the interview, they remember them well and those attributes are the first thing they share when debriefing your interview with others panel members. Ending the interview with the "Closing Question" allows you to strategically bring the interview to a close on a positive note and set you up as the best candidate for the position.

Now It Is Your Turn:

Practice the "Closing Question" below and commit this question to memory. Practice this question with a family member or friend multiple times until you have it both committed to memory and are able to say it confidently and calmly in a live interview setting.

My "Closing Question"

Intro: *"I have one final question. We have had a great conversation today. You have seen my resume and you have heard about some of my skills, experiences and abilities".* **Closing Question:** *"Of all the things you have seen and heard today, what gives you the **most** confidence that I **might** be applicable for this position?"*

<u>Notes</u>

Putting It All Together

Congratulations! You now know the *Ten Keys to Crushing the Interview* and it is time for you to go *Nail* your next interview! In preparation for your next interview, it is time that we take all of these advanced interviewing strategies and put them all together.

10 Keys to Crushing the Interview

1. Frame It Up
2. Give not Get
3. Alignment
4. Short-Long-Short
5. Most & Least
6. Recent & Relevant
7. Failure = Learning
8. Behavioral-Based Answers
9. Front Load
10. Most & Might

The "Stacking Effect"

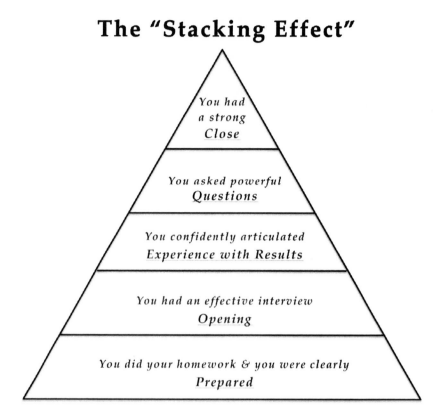

You had
a strong
Close

You asked powerful
Questions

You confidently articulated
Experience with Results

You had an effective interview
Opening

You did your homework & you were clearly
Prepared

When you leverage all Ten Keys to Crushing the Interview and put the "Stacking Effect" at work for you, results are soon to follow and you will land that next opportunity you desire most. Also, as I described in an earlier chapter entitled Preparation is Power, the "Interview Prep Sheet" (see it at the end of this chapter) will help you to focus on the most important elements to consider prior to your next interview. This prep sheet is designed to simply guide you throughout the interview. It is not, however, designed to provide you with the only things you need to prepare for the interview nor is it to provide you with every word you will utilize in the interview. Quite the opposite. I do not encourage any candidate to complete this document utilizing full sentences. Rather, I have found that one or two word bullet points are all that is required for the candidate to successfully navigate this document when referencing it during the interview. Otherwise, it is easy for an applicant to get distracted by all the information on the form and either loses their way or (even worse) get caught in lengthy verbiage and end up reading the document word-for-word to the interviewer. This is a sure-fire way to ensure you do not get the job.

Additionally, you will notice that this document does not contain every single component that we have reviewed in this book. That is because you should reference only a one-page document in the interview with the key items that you must recall. If you would like to include different topics on your "Interview Prep Sheet," you are certainly welcome to do so. However, always keep the "Interview Prep Sheet" to one page. Otherwise, job seekers find themselves shuffling multiple pages in the interview and they appear to be very disorganized and discombobulated when they do so. When this occurs, it has the opposite effect that has negative consequences on the outcome.

The sample "Interview Prep Sheet" that I included below contains the most commonly referenced items during the interview for candidates that I coach and mentor. These items allow the applicant the opportunity to reference the one-to-two word bullet points on the page during the interview, which helps them to stay focused and clear without getting too deep into the details of each item. Each bullet point serves as a simple reminder of the content that the candidate had already prepared in advance of the interview.

Putting it all together allows you to take each of the strategies referenced throughout this book and complete the "Interview Prep Sheet." Here are the key strategies you will want to keep in mind as you complete your own "Interview Prep Sheet."

Key components listed on the "Interview Prep Sheet"

Keys = Key Accomplishments: This section of the prep sheet is designed for you to place a one-to-two words per bullet point that represents the top four items that you want to be sure you reference in your interview. I frequently have job seekers tell me after their interview that they forgot to share a key accomplishment that was critical to set them apart as a candidate for the role (i.e. Masters Degree, saved the company $1.4 million dollars through the initiative they led as a Project Manager, etc.). Remember, for the entire document, you only want to include one or two words per bullet point. Your brain will remember everything else. The bullet points simply serve as a gentle reminder of something you want to be sure to state during the interview..

Frame = Frame It Up: This section simply represents the three items you will reference to answer the question, *"Tell me about yourself,"* which you will answer in 45 seconds or less. Select one word from each of the three items you selected for the frame up that you designed in the chapter entitled *"Frame It Up"* and place those three words in each of the bullet points of this section.

Strengths = Most Beneficial to the New Role: Here you will simply place your three strengths (from your long list of strengths that you outlined in the chapter entitled *"Most & Least"*) that are most beneficial to the new role for which you are applying.

Weaknesses = Least Damaging to the New Role: In this section of the form, you will include your two weaknesses (from your full list of weaknesses that you outlined in the chapter entitled *"Most & Least"*) that are least damaging to the new role for which you are applying.

Success = Recent & Relevant: This bullet is reserved for the success example(s) you outlined in the chapter entitled *"Recent & Relevant."* Remember, the success(es) you select to reference in the interview must be both recent and relevant to the new position you are working to obtain in order to maximize the full benefit of this advanced strategy.

Failure = Learning: This section allows you to record a one-to-two word bullet point that represents the story of a past failure and what you learned as a result, which you identified in the chapter entitled "*Failure = Learning.*" Remember that interviewers are less concerned about the fact that you have had a failure and more interested in what you have learned from that failure that will help you perform better and stronger in your new position when hired.

Questions = "Front Loading": Based on the questions that you developed following the chapter entitled "*Front Load,*" this section provides you with a place to record just one or two word bullet points that will remind you of the data you will share and the questions (three to five is the standard) that you will ask during the interview.

Closing Question = Most & Might: You will notice that this section of the "Interview Prep Sheet" has already been populated with all the verbiage you will need to remind you of the "Closing Question." Be sure to memorize and practice this critical question with friends or family members prior to your next interview.

Four Additional Tips Listed at the Bottom of the Interview Prep Sheet: Last, as a reminder of the four additional keys to crushing the interview, I included the catch phrase from each of the chapters on these subjects. The catch phrases include:

- **"Give Not Get"** (reminding you to answer questions with how you will serve the team and the organization vs. all the benefits you will receive if you get the position.)
- **"Alignment"** (reminding you of the key to answering the question about your plan of action for the first ninety days, which is to align with your boss, your stakeholders, and your direct reports.)

- **"Short-Long-Short"** (reminding you to always end your answer to the short and long-terms goals question by ending with further discussion about your short term goal of performing with excellence in the new role for which you are interviewing for today.)
- **"Have Done not Will Do"** (reminding you to answer hypothetical questions with behavioral-based answers utilizing examples of how you process your thoughts in order to make key decisions.)

One example of a completed "Interview Prep Sheet" that a candidate may use in preparation for their next job interview looks like the following document:

Nailed It!: Ten Keys to Crushing the Interview©: Interview Prep Sheet

Name: _____

Keys
- MBA
- 1.2M
- 17 Dir Reports
- 11 locations

Frame
- Education
- 2 rel roles
- Communication

Strengths
- Results Driven
- Develop Others
- Good Communicator

Weaknesses
- Antsy
- Perfectionist

Success
- Book (recent/relevant)

Failure
- Partnership (learned)

Questions
- 1.2M, opportunity?
- 30%, retention?
- 400, lead?

Closing
- Most Confidence, Might be Applicable

Give not Get, Alignment, Short-Long-Short, Have Done not Will Do

Now It Is Your Turn:

Leveraging all the work you have completed following each chapter to gather information, examples, stories, and data, complete the below blank "Interview Prep Sheet." Then, utilize this "Interview Prep Sheet" to absolutely *"Nail"* your next interview.

Nailed It!: Ten Keys to Crushing the Interview©: Interview Prep Sheet

Name: _____

Keys
-
-
-
-

Frame
-
-
-

Strengths
-
-
-

Weaknesses
-
-

Success
- (recent/relevant)

Failure
- (learned)

Questions
-
-
-

Closing
- Most Confidence, Might be Applicable

Give not Get, Alignment, Short-Long-Short, Have Done not Will Do

HAVE A LITTLE FAITH

The interview process can be challenging. Most people feel a little nervous (some feel overwhelmed with anxiety) as they prepare for their next job interview. What will the interviewer ask? What will they think of me? Will I answer the questions effectively? On and on the questions swirl in our brains putting us in a near state of panic. When this happens, I encourage you to simply have _faith_.

While the advanced interviewing solutions outlined in this book will help you to perform exceptionally well, I also encourage you to have faith as you enter the interviewing process. Have faith in yourself, faith in the process, and faith that you were meant to have this role. Faith has the power to sustain you when you are most nervous and faith can carry you through the most difficult and trying of circumstances. The interview process is no exception.

You have been given unique gifts and amazing talents that are unique to you as a candidate. These are gifts and talents that many organizations will greatly value from when they hire you. And you have impressed someone enough to offer you the opportunity to interview with their organization. Bottom line – you bring something to the table that the organization finds valuable enough to have several leaders pause their daily routine to spend an hour learning more about you, what you have accomplished, and how you can help them to succeed.

Have faith in your skills, your experiences, and your ability to leverage the advanced interviewing solutions that have been outlined for you in this book.

As a result, have faith. Have faith in your skills, have faith in your experiences, and have faith in your ability to leverage the advanced interviewing solutions that have been outlined for you in this book. Go into your next interview with confidence knowing that you have what it takes. Enter your next interview with a spirit of gratitude, knowing that you did not gain all your skills and experiences on your own. Many people have helped and supported you along this journey we call life (teachers, mentors, coaches, co-workers, bosses, clergy, friends, neighbors, family members, and your Creator). Many people have contributed to the successes you have experienced in your career and those same individuals are cheering you on.

The combination of confidence and humility are the "Triumphant Twins" that I mentioned earlier in this book. When you authentically bring these two character strengths into your next interview, they have a profound impact on the outcome. So, interview with faith knowing that you have what it takes to excel at this process and absolutely *nail* your next job interview.

You are not meant to just *survive* the interview.
You are meant to *thrive* in the interview.

As you prepare for your interview, practice the interviewing solutions that you have just read in this book. Prepare your "Interview Prep Sheet" to reference as a guide during your interview. Utilize all *Ten Keys to Crushing the Interview* and leverage "The Stacking Effect" to your advantage. Build a vision for what it will look like and feel like when you are offered the position. Say a prayer and know that God loves you and wants the very best for you. Meditate on the things you have accomplished in your career, and see yourself already celebrating with friends and family after you receive the offer for the job. There is a Proverb that says, "Without a vision, people perish." Most people immediately and logically think this is in reference to physical death. However, I happen to believe that people perish in many ways. I believe people can perish spiritually, emotionally, socially, financially and mentally as well. Create a vision where you see yourself thriving in your new position. See yourself having already won over the interviewers, being offered the job, and already helping the organization to meet all of its goals and objectives.

Last, as part of your interview prep work, plan your celebration in advance. This helps you to build the vision of already having the job and creates the emotions of both confidence and gratefulness that set the best interviewing candidates apart from others. With a clear vision, strong faith, and a plan to celebrate, you are well equipped for every interview you encounter. I am confident you will *crush* each interview you face. Have fun and go in faith with confidence knowing that you will *nail* every interview moving forward. Here's to your success and know that I am cheering you on. All the best to you and your career and remember to interview with passion!

God Bless and Now Go *Nail* Your Next Interview!

ACKNOWLEDGEMENTS

———⌘———

There are so many people to thank for all their help and support in the completion of this project that it is difficult to know where to start and impossible to list them all. Here are just a few.

I want to thank my family (my wife Tammy, my daughter Caila and my son Cole). I appreciate your feedback, insight, and ideas during the writing of this book. Thanks for your patience and continued support. I also want to thank my mom (Deloris Forman) and all my brothers and sisters (Mark Cole, Cheri Runion, Scott Cole, Cathy Cole, Cindy Moore and Lori Paras) who I am grateful to state are also my best friends. I want to thank Ed & Linda Christy (my Father-in-law and Mother-in-law) – Thank you for all your support! I also want to thank my amazing friends Chris & Annie Lowry (Chris, thanks for always finding a way to make me laugh when I am most stressed – you are a gift from God to me) and Jay & Val Ninah (Jay, thanks for all your encouragement and Val for challenging me to move forward with publication). I love you all so much and I thank God every single day for blessing me with the most incredible friends and family. With all the above blessings combined, I am the luckiest man on earth.

I want to thank Tom Toney, CEO of CurrentFamily and Pastor (along with his wife Kathy) at Family.Life.Church. in Marion, Ohio. Tom &

Kathy, your constant encouragement has been a source of energy and strength for me. This book would not be what it is today without your input and expertise. Tom, thank you for the countless hours of editing, the cover design, and your prodding along the way. Even more than all those things, your friendship means the world to me and I am forever grateful for your prayers and support. I also want to thank Victor Toney and Dr. Mary Sue Toney & the entire Toney family to include Dan, Becky, Steve, Debii, Beth & Tom – your lives have impacted my entire extended family and for that I am forever grateful! I also want to thank the many staff members at Family.Life.Church that I have the privilege of working with, which include Casey Watts, Heather Watts, Jeremy & Brittani Dunn, Angie Sayre, Todd & Beth Meadows, Wes & Victoria Meadows, and Jason & Melanie Kwast. I also want to thank the fellow Board Members that I am honored to serve alongside, which include Ric McAllister, Michael Martin, Joe Skiles, and Vernon Deas. For my readers, if you are looking for amazing leaders and speakers who can engage an audience and create real transformation for individuals and for teams, then check out all that Tom & Kathy Toney have to offer at www.currentfamily.com.

I want to thank Keith Lawrence, former P&G HR Executive, Peak Performance Consultant and Co-Author of the Amazon Top 1% Best Selling Book *Your Retirement Quest*. Keith, I so appreciate all your wisdom and advice throughout this process. Thank you for reviewing the book and writing the Foreword. Mostly, my friend, thanks for being in my "front row" cheering me on and helping in more ways that I could ever count. To others, check out Keith's book at www.yourretirementquest. com/buy.php. I promise it will change your life.

I want to thank Steve Toney of Stephen Toney Photography for his amazing talent and generous effort in providing many of the pictures provided in this book. If you're looking for a photographer with the

"X-Factor," check out Stephen Toney Photography on Facebook or on LinkedIn.

I want to thank Lauren Magness, family friend and one of the most talented individuals you will ever meet. Lauren, thank you for all your time and energy to provide the final edits on the book. Please know that you are greatly appreciated!

I want to thank all the clients that I have worked with that have given MGM Consulting permission to utilize their live interviewing video clips during our workshops. Those individuals include Jennifer Lawrence, Patrick Frye, Jason Bruns, Jeff Armada, Monica Burns, Joy Duncan, James Giebler, Brian Spengler, Heinrich Stander, Tom Leonard, Dave Haden, Shariq Tariq, Preston Brown, Jackson Jeffcoat, Kyle Christy, and Jonathan Olsen. Thank you for your commitment to these principles and it has been such an honor to work with so many talented professionals.

I am forever grateful for the team at Xulon Press who helped make this project come to life. I especially want to thank Jennifer Kasper, Jesse Kline, Kimberly Ludwig, Rene Compton, Nick Lopez, and Elizabeth Marrero, all of who put a tremendous amount of time, effort and energy toward this publication. They say "it takes a village" and I am grateful for all that you have done to ensure this book is a success. Check out the great services available and the amazing team to help you publish your next book at www.xulonpress.com.

I want to thank Clif Marshall (Performance Director), Chad Swigert (Business Operations Manager), and the entire staff at Ignition APG in Mason, Ohio. Thanks for your partnership and the work we do together to prepare athletes for their interviews at the NFL Combine each year. I am grateful for your friendship and I appreciate your commitment and support of the "Nailed It!" concepts. The difference Ignition makes for athletes is tremendous and I am forever grateful for the impact this training program has had on my son, Cole. Check out Ignition at www.ignitionapg.com.

I also want to thank the many NFL clients that I have worked with over the years, only a few of which include Jason Kelce (Eagles), John Hughes (Browns), Jackson Jeffcoat (Redskins), Preston Brown (Bills), Jordan Hicks (Eagles), Clayton Geathers (Colts), Darryl Roberts (Patriots), Max Valles (Raiders), Kyle Christy (Free Agent) and the countless others that I have been blessed to work with. It has been my privilege to help you in your journey and may you all have long, healthy, prosperous careers!

I want to thank The Kroger Company and specifically Lynne Rudd and Kim West who were instrumental in providing the initial opportunities for me to facilitate the "Nailed It" advanced interviewing training for the organization. Thanks for your faith and support of this training and it is such a pleasure to work with you both. I also want to thank Mike Purdum for contracting with me for the first executive-level Advanced Interviewing Skills workshop and the attendees, which included Mike Purdum, Steve Zebrasky, Ed Taylor, Jeff Abate, Lynne Rudd, Mark Quertinmont, and Steve King – thanks for your involvement and feedback, which helped to launch additional advanced skills workshops at The Kroger Company for MGM Consulting. One of those workshops includes my Advanced Presentation Skills workshop, and I want to thank David Avery, Lincoln Lutz, Chuck Graefen, Mike Siegert, Jim Klopp, Kirk Ball, Nick Kaufman, Annette Hater, and Jeff Abate – all of whom engaged in these workshops and then rolled them out to their team members. I also want to thank Kevin Edmonds & Tim Massa – I am so grateful to work with an organization that stands for integrity and excellence and it has been my privilege to work with your organization as a consultant throughout the years.

I want to thank Xavier University where I held my first "Nailed It!" workshop on the campus for under-graduate and graduate level students while teaching grad students there as an Adjunct Professor on the campus. Many thanks to Dr. Ida Schick, retired Director/Chair of the Department of Health Services Administration (I'm so grateful for your leadership and your friendship through the years). I would also like to thank Brent Linn of Chick-fil-A for your sponsorship and support of the first "Nailed It!" workshop as well as your partnership during my live satellite teach-back from Jerusalem to my graduate students at Xavier University. I especially want to thank Brenda Levya-Gardner and Sharon Korth of the Xavier University Executive Human Resource Development Masters Degree Program. I was blessed to have you as my professors as part of the XU HRD program Class XVI ("Sweet Sixteen") and I cannot thank you enough for all the inspiration and encouragement you provided along the way. To my XU HRD "Sweet Sixteen" classmates, thanks for the impact you have had on my life and the lifelong friendships that we have formed as a result. I also want to thank Dana Schilling who inspired me to pursue my Masters Degree – I am forever grateful for your encouragement. This program is a must for any Human Resources professional who wants to take their knowledge and skills to a whole new level. Enroll in the program and it will be one of the greatest experiences of your life. Check out Xavier.edu and then Click on "Graduate Programs" and click on "Master of Science in Human Resource Development."

I want to thank the University of Cincinnati for the opportunities to partner with you through the years. I specifically want to thank the UC Center for Corporate Learning to include Cathy Gallenbeck (Sales Executive), Joyce Wagner (Director), and Pete Gemmer (Director of Communications). I also owe a great deal of gratitude to the UC Goering Center and the team of Larry Grypp (President), Steve Hater

(Membership Director), and Mary Beth Hammond (Asst. Director). Thank you for the opportunity to train leaders in your programs over the years and I am grateful for your partnership. For more information about the Goering Center and how they can help your family owned/privately owned business to flourish and grow, log onto www.business. uc.edu/centers/goering.

I am also very grateful for the amazing team at Horizon Leadership in Atlanta, Georgia where I serve as a senior consultant. I especially want to thank Cindy Larkin (CEO) who has been a tremendous source of encouragement and support. Cindy, thank you for your authentic leadership style and I am so grateful for the opportunity we have to serve leaders from all over the globe. I also want to thank Beth Taylor (VP of Operations), Annie Schenck (Director of Talent & Sr. Project Leader), Sarah Mapes (Visual Communications Leader), Lisa Marino-Craig (Relationship & Logistics Manager), Debbie Kizzar (Finance Manager), Amanda Hart (Communications Specialist), and the many talented consultants that I have the privilege of working with at Horizon Leadership. For more information on this game-changing consulting firm, go to www.horizonleadership.com.

I want to thank Chick-fil-A for our consulting partnership over the years. I specifically want to thank Owner/Operators Britton Smith, Dustin DiChiara, Doug Peters, Markus Schleidt, Chuck Perkins, Michael Calloway, Brent Linn, Steve Miller, and Randy Calloway (GM). It has been a privilege to work with you and your teams and I look forward to a long partnership together. I also want to thank several of the Atlanta-based Chick-fil-A team members with whom I've had the privilege of working with through Horizon Leadership, which include Sarah Ketchum (Talent Development Manager) and Diane Paul. I also want to thank Mark Miller (Vice President for Leadership Development for

Chick-fil-A). Mark, your words of encouragement to me as we discussed the book publishing process in Atlanta has impacted me tremendously and I cannot thank you enough for your wisdom and advice. Mark is a brilliant author and you can check out his game-changing books and blogs at greatleadersserve.com.

I want to thank all of my consulting clients for whom I am richly blessed to work with over the years. I especially want to thank Ohio National Financial Services (#1 place to work in Cincinnati 4 of the past 5 years) and the amazing leaders that I have the privilege of working with, which include Gary T. "Doc" Huffman (CEO), Debby Combs (Director of Talent Management), Tony Esposito (Sr. VP & Chief Human Resources Officer), Pam Webb (VP of Human Resources), Traci Nelson (VP & Program Manager), Chris Eversole (Manager of Talent Development and Recruitment), Justin Miller (Talent Development and Recruitment Administrative Assistant) and Jessica Snipes (Talent Development Specialist) who always provide outstanding support for every training program we provide. Thank you for your partnership and I look forward to many great years to come for Ohio National Financial Services! I also want to thank Ryan Hartsock (Creative Director of The Underground and Co-Founder/Producer for Paper Ghost Pictures) who provided all the video support for the training at Ohio National. I also want to thank GE and the entire Crotonville Learning & Development Management Team for the opportunity to teach and train many of the leadership team members through the skills courses that I have facilitated at GE over the years. I want to thank Miller Valentine (top place to work in Cincinnati, Ohio) and specifically Carol Bise (Director of Human Resources) who has been a tremendous business partner and friend. I love working with you and your staff and I appreciate the privilege of working with the talented leadership team at your organization. I want to thank RICOH and specifically Allison Adams (Principal Consultant), Karen Henry (Principal Consultant), and Tracy Pickel (Director, US Project Management Office). You are so wonderful to work with and I greatly appreciate your partnership. I would also like to thank Cincinnati Children's Hospital Medical Center (specifically Wendy Steuerwald, Clinical Manager of Audiology), Cincinnati/ Northern Kentucky International Airport (specifically Debby Shipp, Sr. Manager of Organizational Development), BASCO (specifically Jim Brockschmidt (Director of Human Resources), George Rohde (CEO & President), and Brad Michaelson (Customer Service Manager) as well as the countless other clients that I work with every day, which range from Universities and Non-Profit organizations to family-owned/privately-owned companies and large multi-national corporations. It has been such an honor to serve you and your organization and I am grateful for all your encouragement and support.

I also want to thank Gap Inc. (Gap, Old Navy, Banana Republic, Athleta), who provided me with the opportunity to exercise my recruiting skills at a completely new level. I want to thank Tim Haran, Steve Biondo, Bruce Gulley, Steve Hopper, Lisa Danahy and Dana Schilling (all of whom I reported to at one point in my tenure with the company). Thank you all for your belief in me as well as your coaching, mentorship, and support. I also want to thank Shawn Curran who provided a great deal of encouragement and coaching during the various roles that I held at Gap Inc. The impact that all of these individuals have had on my career is tremendous and has shaped me into who I am today.

I want to thank The Longaberger Company for the opportunity to be involved with this amazing organization. I'll never forget my final conversation with Dave Longaberger, who impacted so many people and influenced generations of artisans (Dave, you will forever be in our hearts!). I want to thank Tom Coles, who supported my efforts and helped to pave a way for me at The Longaberger Company. I also want to thank Tami Longaberger for her support of my role at the company and the privilege of working with some of the most authentic people on the planet.

I would like to thank Kings Island Amusement Park near Cincinnati, Ohio and the opportunity I had to lead the recruiting, employment, and training functions for the company. I specifically want to thank Bill Ossim, Don Miller and Dave Greenberg for believing in me and giving me the opportunity to impact people in a positive way.

I want to thank Bowling Green State University, where I achieved my undergraduate degree in Interpersonal and Public Communication with a minor in Psychology. I am so grateful that I received my undergraduate degree from BGSU and I am so thankful for all the opportunities you provided me with along the way. I specifically want to thank Dr. Richard Weaver, Dr. R.K. Tucker (whom I published my first work with at Bowling Green), and Dr. Randy Pruitt. You had a huge impact on the direction of my career and I am forever grateful! It was at Bowling Green State University that I first began studying the art of interviewing and the passion for this subject has only grown stronger. Check out my alma mater and discover endless possibilities for expanding your knowledge at BGSU.edu.

I want to thank the Southwestern Sales and Leadership Program located in Nashville, Tennessee. How do I even begin to thank you for the doors your program has opened up for me through the years?! The sales training your organization provided me with is second to none and I attribute much of the business success I have achieved over the years to your program. The lifelong friendships (including Sean Lewis, Julie Tobin-Homes, Tim Holmes, Angie Hensel, Julie Perles-Fisher, and countless others) have meant the world to me and I learned the equivalent of a

'Masters Degree' from the Southwestern training and work opportunities. If you are a college student looking for an amazing experience and the best resume builder on planet earth, then check out southwestern.com and click on "southwestern advantage."

I want to thank Upper Sandusky High School. I am so grateful to have graduated from USHS and the experiences that I gained there (everything from being a Captain of the Track Team and playing Wide Receiver for the Upper Rams to being the President of *Students Against Drunk Driving*, the President of *Fellowship of Christian Athletes*, and the Lead in *Joseph and the Amazing Technicolor Dreamcoat* directed in 1986 by the late Alan Walton (Alan, you will forever be in our hearts!). I also want to thank teacher extraordinaire Jan Stoneburner, who was a source of never ending encouragement (I still have your note that you wrote on one of my speech papers – "One day I will get to say 'I was his teacher...'"). My consulting career is heavily influenced by your teaching and your speech coaching ... thank you!

Given the fact that all these amazing people have played such an important part in my life, I am (among all men) most richly blessed!

About the Author

Matthew G. Marvin, M.Ed. is President & CEO of MGM Consulting, a Cincinnati-based consulting firm that provides leadership development, executive coaching, and organizational effectiveness for Fortune 100 companies worldwide.

Matthew is a professional speaker who provides many keynote speeches for countless conferences across the globe. Matthew has experience that reaches across many industries and ranges from one-on-one executive coaching with C-Suite Leaders and teaching Executive Leaders of multi-billion dollar corporations to small group facilitation and large-scale conferences for corporations, universities, and non-profits. He teaches leaders at numerous companies that range from General Electric and The Kroger Company to Chick-fil-A and RICOH. Matthew has a passion for training and development and has also served as an Adjunct Professor for graduate students at Xavier University and taught Executive Members of the University of Cincinnati Goering Center.

Matthew has international experience that spans the globe, to include working with individuals and teams in the United States, Canada, London, Scotland, Germany, India, Africa, China, Japan, Jamaica, & Israel. He holds a Master's Degree in Executive Human Resources Development from Xavier University and a Bachelor's Degree in Interpersonal & Public Communications with a minor in Psychology from Bowling Green State University.

With over 20 years as a Human Resources leader, Matthew has developed and implemented breakthrough strategies in the areas of Training & Development, Individual and Team Performance, Organizational Development, and Leadership Effectiveness. Matt's areas of expertise include executive coaching, training & development, organizational dynamics, team coaching, group facilitation, change management, and both individual & team performance.

Certifications: Matthew is certified in Emotional Intelligence (Hay Group), Situational Leadership II (Ken Blanchard Consulting), DiSC (Center for Internal Change), 360° Feedback Coaching (Lominger), Change & Transition Management (William Bridges Model), Myers-Briggs, and Time Management.

Services Available

Matthew Marvin can be contacted regarding the following services:

- Large Scale Auditorium-Style Conferences
- 1:1 Executive Coaching
- Training & Development for organizations and in-tact teams
- Organizations who are experiencing large scale change
- Workshops for College and University students

MGM Consulting is available for both one-on-one coaching and/or group facilitation. Many leaders are interested in one-on-one coaching and may contact our organization to establish individual coaching sessions that include resume building, video-taped before and after interviewing coaching sessions, and personalized coaching sessions prior to and/or following his interview workshops.

We also have organizations (companies, colleges, non-profits, outplacement agencies, etc.) who are interested in our master facilitators providing group training and coaching for multiple employees/clients. During these sessions, we can also offer video-taped sessions, mock interviews, and resume building workshops.

Last, Matthew Marvin can also provide key note speeches, large group trainings, and one-on-one coaching on a variety of subjects listed in this bio.

Additional Workshops That MGM Consulting Facilitates include:
- Nailed It! 10 Keys to Crushing the Interview ©
- Behavioral Based Interviewing: Truths & Myths
- Resume Writing on Steroids ©
- Impact: Advanced Presentation Skills ©
- Bullets, Bouncy Balls & Barriers: Two Primary Mindsets in the Workplace ©
- Strengths Based Leadership
- Meeting Mastery ©
- Situational Leadership II
- Client Engagement & Buy-in
- Time Optimization ©
- The Everest Simulation
- DiSC & Myers Briggs
- Myers-Briggs
- Performance Coaching and Feedback
- Decision Making and Problem Solving
- Emotional Intelligence
- Change Management
- Five Dysfunctions of a Team
- True North
- Team Building
- GPS: Navigating Your Own Career ©
- High-Po to Promo ©
- iLead © Training Series: Eight ½-day sessions for Senior Leaders

For those interested in contacting MGM Consulting for additional services, please go to www.matthewgmarvin.com or send an email to MGM Consulting at matthewgmarvin@gmail.com. We are always happy to serve you and your organization and we will look forward to hearing from you soon.

Here's To Your Success!

Matthew G. Marvin
President/Owner
MGM Consulting
www.mathewgmarvin.com

CPSIA information can be obtained at www.ICGtesting.com
Printed in the USA
BVOW02*2242230715

410084BV00002B/60/P